DWELLING SELLING:

How the Internet Made Selling a House in the South Bay Easy and Other Funny Stories

DARYL PALMER

JONES MEDIA
PUBLISHING

Jones Media Publishing
10645 N. Tatum Blvd. Ste. 200-166
Phoenix, AZ 85028
www.JonesMediaPublishing.com

Book cover photo credit: Paul M. Towers

Printed in the United States of America

Disclaimer:

The author strives to be as accurate and complete as possible in the creation of this book, notwithstanding the fact that the author does not warrant or represent at any time that the contents within are accurate due to the rapidly changing nature of the Internet.

While all attempts have been made to verify information provided in this publication, the Author and Publisher assume no responsibility and are not liable for errors, omissions, or contrary interpretation of the subject matter herein. The Author and Publisher hereby disclaim any liability, loss or damage incurred as a result of the application and utilization, whether directly or indirectly, of any information, suggestion, advice, or procedure in this book. Any perceived slights of specific persons, peoples, or organizations are unintentional.

In practical advice books, like anything else in life, there are no guarantees of income made. Readers are cautioned to rely on their own judgment about their individual circumstances to act accordingly. Readers are responsible for their own actions, choices, and results. This book is not intended for use as a source of legal, business, accounting or financial advice. All readers are advised to seek services of competent professionals in legal, business, accounting, and finance field.

ISBN-13: 978-1-945849-63-3 paperback
JMP2018.4

CONTENTS

INTRODUCTION

A book about Real Estate? Really?

IT SEEMS THAT the newest "fancy word" or "buzzword" out there is "disruptors." (I prefer to say "fancy word"… it's my favorite.) In the real estate industry, the current disruptors are the big real estate websites that you already know about. They're getting into the real estate biz and trying to buy and sell your house. I know … shocking! Also, the Internet has changed the way we do our real estate business. Mostly in the last couple of years! This is amazing to watch. It's fun! Really! I like change. I also like that most of my fellow real estate agents do not like change. This is why it's fun! Thus … this book. So much disrupting!

This book is about how the way we market and communicate has drastically changed because of the Internet. Also how overly regulated and ridiculous things have become. Thank you for being here to read it. It's quite entertaining and informative, all while being totally ridiculous.

To change and the disruptors! I welcome you with open arms. Because real estate cannot be taken over completely by robots*.*see end of Chapter 6

Inside these pages (well, probably on top of these pages where all the ink is) you'll learn what you need to do to sell your house here in the South Bay. How to locate a smart agent (Hint: my contact info is on the back). How to price a property and how not to. How to market it for maximum results. What the meaning of DOM, PPF, OTB and HTCS are, and what they mean to you. You'll learn a fun game to play at parties. Also you'll realize that I like to use three dots at end of sentences ... or in the middle of sentences ... rather than figure out how to make said sentences more concise ... this is all part of the highly technical "Daryl's Relaxed Conversational Style" which is where you, the reader, feels like you are in a "relaxed" conversation with me, the famous author. And when I say "conversation", it's more like a one-sided conversation, because I'm doing all the talking. And when you make comments out loud, and say things like, "Good one, Daryl! Keep going!" or "That was funny, old chap! You're the best!" ... I simply cannot hear them.

Nevertheless, when you're done, you'll be a lot smarter and much more exhausted than when you started, and you'll probably need a nap or a martini... or both. So go pour a martini. And while you're here ... you must at least read Chapter One. Write On!

To give you even more confidence in my authoring skills. My sophomore English teacher, Granny Davidson, once mentioned to me that I was one of the worst writers she'd seen in her 92 years of teaching. She finished her lecture by saying: "You will NEVER write anything that people would want to read!"

I guess she was write.

CHAPTER 1

"Don't believe everything you read on the Internet." – Abraham Lincoln

G REETINGS! HOME OWNERSHIP is a fabulous thing! Everyone should own at least one home, unless you have a really good reason not to … like, if you're in the fourth grade, or if you live on a polar icecap and are forced to build shelters from huge ice blocks. Jimmy Buffet (or Warren Beatty or someone with a similar name) said more millionaires have been made by owning real estate than any other investment. If Jimmy or Warren can do it, then you should too!

Let's recap the book so far.

    A.   Home ownership can be profitable.
    B.   Jimmy Warren is very famous.
    C.   Ice-block living is not for you.

Now let's skip to the end. Congratulations! You own a home! Jimmy and Warren and your mom are very proud of you! Good job. Now you need to get rid of it. What to do? Selling a home in the digital age in Southern California is much different now than it was even a handful of years ago. (How many years are in a handful, you ask? See the chart on page 221.) Well, first you check Robot-zillo, and you see what the robot says your home is worth. Then you run into Bobby, the know-it-all guy at work, and ask his opinion. (He is, in fact, an expert because he watches all the HGTV shows and loves that *Trillion Dollar Listing* show.)

Then you consider hiring your neighbor's friend Bobbi, who "has a real estate license" but doesn't use it. Or maybe you find the agent who will only charge you $500 to sell your $2 million dollar house because "real estate agents make too much money." Yes! You're on to something! If you live where I do, in the South Santa Monica Bay (we call it the South Bay ... you can call it whatever you want), there's a crazy thing nearby that affects values in varying ways. You've probably seen it; it's that silly body of water west of us called the Specific Ocean, or as Fozzie Bear calls it, the "Big, Blue Wet Thing." It's amazing that a body of water can disrupt so many things. Real estate values can vary widely, even on the same street if one house has views of the ocean and the other doesn't.

These are exactly the kinds of things the robots don't know. Another thing that the Big, Blue Wet Thing disrupts is driving! Imagine you're driving west on Manhattan Beach Boulevard. There's a point where you simply cannot drive any further west. Why? That damn ocean! There are no roads! (Yes, I did graduate from University.) Anyway, I'm glad you're here. If you weren't here, then where else would you be? Keep reading for an eyes-wide-shut view of the how to really sell a property. Or maybe it's an eyes-wide-open view, I can't remember which.

Okay, so how did you get here? We either met at an open house or someone gave you this book because they felt you needed it. Or perhaps you saw it on Amazon, on the Interwebs or through an infomercial at 3 a.m. on the Book Shopping Network? You may not think you need me, but after you read this book – or even if you only read two chapters – you will! (When I say "me," I mean "me and this book," and when I say "two chapters," I mean "13 or 14".) This is your handbook to at least help you have an understanding of what it takes to sell a property; because selling a house today is HARD! When you're in the middle of selling, it can be really overwhelming. Carry this book with you always.

Not only are there four million pieces of paper inside a real estate transaction, there are multiple personalities involved! Think about this: Every transaction is different. Every property, location, and condition is different. There's me ... I'm an agent with 30-plus years of experience. I do things my way ... because it works for me and my clients. Then there's possibility of another agent representing the other side, and they do things their way, right or wrong. Then there's a loan officer, a title rep, the escrow team, and the other buyer or seller. If you're lucky, maybe there's more than two of them, plus John, your sister's brother-in-law, "advising you," albeit incorrectly because he sold a house 10 years ago, so he knows ... right?

You get the picture. Every party in a transaction has its "way." Some people are nice, some are not nice. But how do YOU work with these types of people? For instance, let's say you're confronted with an over negotiator (I call them junior negotiators, Or JR's. Or JRS negotiators, for short). They think they need to negotiate every little detail and even every conversation and WIN every time. How do you work with, and around that personality? Fun, right? How do you work around the mounds of disclosures and reports? The home inspections, the loan processes, appraisal glitches, closing delays, pushy real estate agents, aggressive Girl Scout cookie salespeople. ... Anyway, you see where I'm going with this, right? Not yet? No worries! You're doing great! Keep going.

You need ME, someone with a ton of experience in babysitting and using sugar before lemons. What's that you say? Sugar? Lemons? Real estate? You know there are multiple ways to say something: You can say the same thing using different words and different inflections and different timing and get vastly different results. Sugar seems to always work better than lemons. Speaking of lemons, I simply do not like those lemon Girl Scout cookies no matter how many boxes I'm forced to purchase. I'm a professional problem solver. That's all I do, every day. There's always a snag that comes up and we as agents must solve it or the seller – you – or the buyer won't get what they want.

Simply put, I use sandpaper to smooth out the rough edges. I don't cut corners, I smooth them. Sometimes I have to bring the banjo out and play a tune for everyone. (I just wrote that ridiculous sentence just to see if you're still reading this. Don't be silly, I traded my banjo for a Strat in the '90s.) More about me later. Let's get on to the good stuff.

This book is a sequence of words that are both meaningful and meaningless that hopefully has a laugh at the end. Next Chapter!

CHAPTER 2

Where Are You Going, and How Soon Do You Need to Be There?

I "hope" I'll Be Home for Christmas ... or Festivus ... or Whatever

THIS IS A new chapter, so I guess we'll call this Chapter Two... So you own a house and you need to sell it. Now what? Well, you've already checked Zillow, right? They sent you an evaluation of your house and you're either 1- mad or 2- giddy.

Zillow knows your house, right? Your improvements. Redfin knows your view, doesn't it? Trulia knows your neighbor backs up to commercial land and you don't, right? Wait, don't they? Unfortunately for you, the robots don't know anything about anyone's house except the price and the square footage, divided by 7.3725 ... voila! (I always thought that word was pronounced with a 'V' like in 'violin,' or 'viola' ... whoops!) Has this happened to you yet? If not, it's in your near future. You're going to finish reading this sentence and go check out what Zilly has to say. If you live in the South Bay, then you know it's all about how far to the beach and if you have a view. Well, that's not all. There's always "How close are you to an Irish bar?" It's very important if you're in a coastal community in SoCal.

NAR states that more than 95% of people looking to buy or sell a home rely on the internet as the MAIN source of information. Yes... MAIN source. Two years ago that was less than 50%.

I recently had a client who Zillowed and came up with $2.65 million as a price for their house. Then, a recent refinance appraiser, (see the later chapter about appraisers,) came in with a value of $2.8 million. When I showed the seller the actual data – recent sales in the last 90 days of comparable properties in their neighborhood – the price was more in the neighborhood of $2.35-$2.4 million. We priced the house at $2.4 million. After 10 days in the market, we got four offers, all at $2.4 million. No one went over that value. Who knows real estate values? Hmmm, hmmm, hmmm. Picture me scratching my head.

After being "Zillowed" or visited by a uniformed appraiser, I show up. During our first meeting, you might think I'm an idiot ... perhaps like the typical "lying real estate agent" trying to underprice everything so I can make a commission. That's the first day. I call this process "getting Zillowed." After a couple of weeks on the market, I look like a genius. How does that happen? Thirty years experience in selling real estate may just very well help me be "Smarter Than A Robot". (I do want to be on that show, by the way.) We've learned in the movies to never piss off or embarrass a robot, right? It just always gets messy after that. Ask Will Smith, he knows firsthand. Okay, so you check Zilly and have a "possible range of value," albeit a very large possible range. Then what?

"Daryl who?" - Will Smith

When I say "possible range," It's really a polite jab at what I'm really going to say. A Zilly-Est is usually much higher than what the market is ... or way lower. The takeaway is that you just can NEVER trust a robot. <u>Call a human</u>. Call a human named Daryl Palmer who wrote this book for you to you stay away from any robot danger. You call a Real-tor!

We're pausing here: Realtor… Only two syllables … NEVER work with a real estate agent who cannot correctly pronounce their own profession. This is nuts, but more than half of my fellow Realtors cannot correctly say the word Realtor. It's a two-syllable word. If you hear three, walk away. It's pronounced Realtor with a long 'O'. Easy, just like its spelled.

It's not real-ter, by the way. The 'O' is a direct giveaway of using the 'O' sound. You've also heard it this way: real-uh-ter or real-uh-der. What? If I'm in a profession and I simply cannot or will not pronounce the name of my own profession correctly, doesn't that tell you something about said "professional"? If I'm a doctor and I tell you I'm a doc-uh-ter or I'm a lawyer and I tell you I'm a loy-uh-yer, would you work with me? Shouldn't your confidence level with these people crumble when they can't correctly pronounce their own profession? It's the weirdest thing ever. Now if YOU pronounce it incorrectly, that's ok. I'll try to coach you in the meantime. Yet how could YOU be expected to pronounce it correctly when the alleged professionals don't either? If you're a civilian, I have no judgment. If you're an alleged pro, well you should learn a new word today.

Anyway, moving on … you have a house … you need to sell it. I show up and we start a dialog that will start us crafting a plan, a strategy, and a plan of attack that has roughly four-and-a-half million moving parts. I'll ask you questions like the following, (this is where you should get out a pen and paper and start making a list.) Where are you going? When do you need to be there? What if you overprice your house and it doesn't sell? What is your plan B … your plan C? Are you moving up? Scaling down? What about your job, family, midlife, midwife, did you just win the lottery? Etc. Your answer determines how we start a plan. Do you need to sell *this* house to buy *that* one? Do you mind putting your stuff in storage and renting something for a short time? What is your favorite Girl Scout cookie? And so on.

Why would I need to know all that, you ask? Because it's very difficult to manage to sell one house and purchase another if you're using the proceeds from the sale to fund the purchase. It all depends on the "market" – seller's market versus buyer's market, multiple offers versus higher DOM. Shop talk! When do you need to be there? Is it a transfer? Does this have to coincide with timing of a school year starting or new job starting; will a spouse remain at the old house? Is it fine if the family separates for a while? Also, do you have issues with cats, larger rodents or white chocolate? This is very important to know in advance!

I've had several families get stuck in this zone, some kind of transfer. One spouse goes to a new city. Let's say it's Elko, Nevada. The other spouse stays, with the kids in school, waiting for an offer on the house. This transferee seller – let's call him Bobby – he got some bad advice. Guy on a plane or a neighbor, or maybe he even got Zillowed and overpriced his house. Bobby is in Elko for a couple of months. The kids don't remember what he looks like after a while. He develops a gambling problem because the casino in town has the best seafood buffet. You see how this can go. Tick, tick, DOM marches on. Bobby just needs an offer or a better plan C. Don't be a Bobby!

What if your house doesn't sell? I'm going to just come out and say it: What if you OVERPRICE your house and it doesn't sell? Well, you can regroup, update the comparable sales and be more realistic. You can finally decide to pack up your massive ceramic cat creamers collection that is blocking the front door, or you could buy a bunch of St. Joseph home sale kits from Amazon – he IS the patron saint of real estate transactions, after all – and really get serious.

What's your plan B? Are you stuck on a value we've found that is simply too high? You really like that number, it sounds nice. In fact, you've already spent some of that money. Of course, it's my fault that it hasn't sold, right? It's also my fault you don't like white chocolate! And what the heck is DOM?

If you did everything I advised you to do, then this part almost never happens. Why, you ask? Why does it never happen? Because I would have told you that you're overpriced and that we need to reduce your price in order to find the market. See how easy this can be?

Okay, plan B. What is it? You might also want a plan C because if the plan B was crafted as well as your plan A ...overprice it because I need the money ... then your plan B may not work either, so plan C, yes! That's where some reality comes in and you start making better judgments. Because by now, DOM is pounding at the door and you're the only one who still thinks your house is worth that lovely number.

At this point you're probably saying, "Wow! This could take a while. And what the heck IS DOM?" Great question! And you're right, it could take a while.

Moving on ... How's the market? Well, that answer will depend on several things. Are you a seller or a buyer? What price point are you at? Where? What area? What neighborhood? What is it? Single-family house, townhome, condo, multi-family, new construction, tear-downs. Are you a cash buyer, or are you financing the purchase? Are you putting the minimum down? Are you putting a lot down? Are you moving up or scaling down? Or are you wanting to perhaps move away from that pesky neighbor who's always peering into your windows?

If you're a seller, you have to know all of these things. Believe it or not, there's an entire submarket in each one of those parameters. (Unless the market is really crappy, then everything is probably really crappy.) All of those things are reversed if you're a buyer. Unless, of course, the market is crappy.

Now, go get a notepad and a pen and keep going! (**Everyone** knows you don't sell a house with a pen and paper. I'm obviously trying to weed out the overachievers who are massive list writers.)

PPF and The Interwebs Changed Everything

Where We Learn Acronyms are Fun AND Profitable!

You made it this far, you might as well keep going!

IT COULD TAKE two to six months from start to finish ... really! From the time we first started the conversation, it could take one to four weeks just to get your house ready for the market. Shocking... right? I bet you know someone – or you are that someone – who hired an agent, they plant a sign in the yard on the first day and you never saw them again. And I'm sorry, that's so 20th-century marketing, man! Welcome to the 21st. Things have changed. Technology has changed everything. I have developed a multi-spoked marketing wheel. It's big and brawny. Talk about a lot of moving parts and pieces. Sheesh! What was I thinking?

I call it "Pre-Planning Fun," or PPF (see what I did there?), and you'll agree it is fun. Painting, fixing, decluttering, who? Us? Staging. (Relax; their stuff probably looks better than your stuff.) Pre-inspecting, web marketing, pre-marketing, custom sign creation, website building, video planning, shooting, editing and posting, planning social media strategies, flyers, postcards, and door-knocking around the house, just to start.

IF YOU PRE-INSPECT ... YOU WILL DEFLECT. Let's start with pre-inspections. Why? Well, every property needs something. Every property has a "list". Even if you think there's nothing wrong with your house, guess what? There's going to be a "list".

There are things hiding and lurking that have broken or stopped working, or started leaking. I'm currently working with a couple who is buying a brand-new house. The inspection came up with more than 40 items that needed addressing. Forty items! I'm the house with Bonnie and Toby and the inspector, doing his inspection thing, he fills the upstairs bathtub. Five minutes later, half of the downstairs has water on the floor. Brand-new house! Every property has a "list." NAR, the National Association of Realtors, says 65 percent of sales that didn't close escrow were stemming from inspections. ... In other words, the property had problems.

If a deal crashes at the inspection period, the property has a lot of problems. Or maybe the seller – let's call him Bobby again – decided he's not going to do a single thing to his $2.5 million house. The buyer can have it as-is. Dude. Wait, so you're netting $2 million and you're going to tell the people who are giving you that $2.5 million to stick it? Great move! I bet you're fun at Christmas as well! Shocking? This happens. A lot!

"IF YOU PRE-INSPECT ... YOU WILL DEFLECT." --Daryl Palmer

In just about every real estate market, investing in something like repainting the house inside and out, or minor repairs, for instance, can increase the value and create fewer objections a future buyer may have. So let's say the house needs paint. In our communities, it may cost $15,000-45,000 to paint it, in real dollars. A buyer will think it costs $50,000-70,000. Same thing with a worn-out roof, appliances or flooring. Buyers generally think repairs cost twice what they actually cost. They usually don't know, so they're guessing.

Most people don't even know what it costs to replace a roof? Or, just off the top of your head, how much does it cost to remove wallpaper and repair and repaint seven bedrooms and thirteen bathrooms? How much does it cost to fumigate and tent a house to treat for termites? How much does it cost to remove the clown troupe living in the attic? According to Pillar and Posts website (the home inspectors franchise), they say for every $1,000 of perceived repair, buyers will ask for $3,000- $5,000 in repair or price reduction. Do the math! It's Money in the Bank if you handle the large portions of the 'list' before going to market!

See what I mean? There you have it, and going back to an inspection during the transaction, if the "list" seems insurmountable to one or both of the parties, the deal gets canceled. A buyer walks, seller has to put it back in the market, and guess what's been happening the two weeks you're in escrow doing inspections? DOM ... tick ... tick ... tick.

We pre-inspect ... we will deflect. It's smart. Yes, it costs $400-800. Remember the $2 million profit? Step into it, Mr. Buffet. ... Okay, never mind. Doing an inspection is part of my marketing suite. I pay for it, because I know you don't want to. You don't think it's necessary. You don't want to deal with any repairs that show up on your "list." Maybe you don't want to know so you don't have to disclose things, but more on that later. No matter how perfect you think your house is, or how impeccably maintained you've kept it, I know we'll find stuff wrong and you'll get to fix it *without* a demanding buyer and their agent and **DOM**. We'll be able to make a plan on what to fix and get it done in *our* timeframe. You'll take care of most of the 42 items on your "list" *prior* to market (remember when I said it could take some time to even get it on to the market?). We haven't even talked about your extensive cat creamer collection!

If your house needs paint, you'll net more money faster if you paint it before you hit the market. Remember actual cost versus what a buyer thinks it cost? Let's say Bobby is dying to move to Barstow, but first he needs to sell his house in Manhattan Beach. He doesn't believe me when I tell him that he'll sell it for more moola if he paints it and pre-inspects it. Why doesn't he believe me? Well, he obviously knows more about selling real estate than me and he sold many more homes than I have, right? Or maybe it just hasn't been the same since that fall off the ladder last Columbus Day*.

*Now 'Indigenous Peoples Day'. By the way, do any of us care about Columbus and the three little ships- El Nino, The Pinto and The Santa Monica anyway? And why three *little* ships?

Chapter three, quiz one, question one: What do you call a house that needs paint and has at least 42 items on the "list?"

- A. A fix-up
- B. A handyman special
- C. A house on *Fix or Flop*
- D. All of the above

Question number two, what do you call a house that's been recently repainted and has just a few minor items showing up on home inspection?

- A. Well maintained
- B. Move-in ready
- C. Both A and B

How did you do on the quiz? If you got two correct, good job! You can move on. If you got one correct, good job! You're almost there. Try a few cleansing breaths and retake the test. If you got both wrong, good job! Try starting this chapter over and maybe a little less day drinking (or more?).

Okay, we pre-inspect. We get the "list." We look at the "list," and you take care of the big items. We leave the small stuff. We don't need to do *everything*. Now, when you get an offer, the buyer does an inspection and has a few minor things on the list ... but definitely not 42. The buyer feels they are minor items and maybe asks for them to be done, or you can give them a small credit at close of escrow and leave it to them to take care of it later. Also, this is going to depend on the current market. If the market is crappy, yeah, you're going to do those repairs. If the market's crazy sailing and you had multiple offers, maybe not.

This right here is what I call the "Second Negotiation".

Reading from:

> The Book of Negotiations, Chapter 2, verses 10-24 states, "*If thou sayeth nay to thine Realtors' expert counsel and thou putteth thine home on the market with nary a spec of paint nor repair, then thou shalt call down from the heavens the fury of the Second Negotiation unto thine self and it shall cost thou many thousands of shekels, or the entire sale, whichever cometh first. And thou doest deserveth nay, none rewards. For I toldeth thou soeth*"

If I can help you understand PPF, then you'll see the value of some pre-planning, hitting the market strong and virtually eliminating the

Second Negotiation, and thus having a much higher chance of a successful closing.

Remember NAR? They tell us of all the transactions that fall out of escrow, more than 65 percent fail during the inspection period due to something the inspectors have noted that either scared off the buyers or caused the buyers to ask for repair or credit for the repair that the seller wasn't interested in doing. This happens every day kids, all the time, all over the world. Yet, most agents won't tell you about it and offer a solution. Why? You ask? Good question! You get an offer and there's an inspection and the buyer sends a long "list" of things to repair. You tell the buyer you're not interested in their repair list. They cancel. Just like that, they're gone.

How much time has gone by? A couple of weeks? More? Remember **DOM**? PPF versus **DOM**?

Chapter three, quiz two, question one.

What the heck is **DOM**?

- A. Daring Ops Mission
- B. Dogs Over Manhattan
- C. Darling Opera Monkey
- D. Days On Market

If you chose A, good job! But it's not A, it's D, **Days On Market**. See it now? By a raise of hands, who here was paying attention earlier and knew that already? Yes! I see that hand. You're on a roll! **Days On Market** ... it's UNFORGIVING! It keeps ticking, not caring if you have an offer and your buyer is in their contingency period (when we're waiting for the buyer to do inspections, get the appraisal and wait for final loan approval, the whole deal is hinging on the "contingency period"). Everything is unsure until all contingencies are lifted... tick ... tick ... If contingencies are NOT lifted and the deal gets cancelled, and after you get both parties to sign the mutual cancellation ... a couple more days ... tick ... tick ... then you're back on the market ... and you're showing 32 **DOM**! Yikes! After 30 days or so, everyone starts asking, "What's wrong with the house?" Or saying, "Of course it's not selling, it's overpriced." Even if you originally got a full price offer! Yeah! The Interwebs baby!

The internet changed everything. Go ahead and blame Al Gore: He invented it, so it really is his fault. Here we are in a digital world moving closer to real robots and self-driving cars. No, thanks. I want my '65 Mustang, please, with a carburetor and a four-speed. We're in it though, and it's bearing down on us. Every day there's something new: some new phone, 30 new apps, new software that changes everything we knew yesterday. When I started selling real estate, we didn't have "computers." We had a terminal. (Think typewriter with NCR paper in it.) What's NCR paper? If you don't know, then Google it.

We had to type search codes into this thing and it would print out a four-line description, almost no details about the properties. Four lines of description for a house. Maybe 40 words. Sounds fun, doesn't it? When we finally got our codes right, we hit print. We had no idea if there was 1 house, 0 houses or 400 on this list. It printed backward and forward across the page, one line at a time. It took forever, but not as long as looking through the MLS books that came out every Friday. We kept those in the back seat of our car with our Thomas Bros. Map Book. Again, you can Google that. Those MLS books were fancy, with a grainy two-inch by two-inch picture of the house. When I say 'fancy', I mean they were terrible, but they were all we had when we were out in a car. Also a fun fact, we didn't have cell phones yet either. We used PAY PHONES! (Just Google it, kids.)

Sometimes you couldn't tell what it was a picture of. Was it a house, or a tree? Something else entirely? There were six listings on a page, kind of like old-school phone books. It was brutal. Back then, we didn't know **DOM**, we had to guess based on the MLS number. When people walked into an open house, they knew nothing about the house and they asked me questions about it and they actually listened. Those were the good old days! Ha ha. Now, when I'm holding an open house, people walk in and they know the price and the year built, they've seen all the pictures online, and know if the price has been reduced. You know what else they know? **DOM**.

... Tightly gripping the <u>Book of Negotiations</u>

If that **DOM** number is high, guess what they ask me first? "What's wrong with this house? It's been on the market for 102 days. What's up with that?" See why I spent so many paragraphs talking about you-know-what? (Hint: it's **DOM**). It's a thing; man ... a big, big thing ... and old-schoolers don't get it. They're still doing things the same way we did them 20 years ago. Guess what? Real estate is changing every day. If you can't keep up, later dude! **DOM** is a cruel, punishing thing for those who don't believe in the magic genie known as PPF*. I'm a believer! (Said loudly in a TV-preacher tone with hand in the air ... tightly gripping the <u>Book of Negotiations</u> ... in a sustainable way). *Pre Planning Fun

See? I mentioned earlier that there are some things we need to talk about – and plan around – before we go to market. It's not just planting a sign out front; there's a lot to do. Problem is, most people think their home is worth more than it is. I call it being Zillowed. Most people lack understanding of current market values and market environment conditions. How could I expect you to be an expert on the current real estate market here? Don't ask Zilly. What do you do if you overprice it? This is when you reveal your plan B and plan C. Ta-da!

If you don't want to spend time upfront, you could be spending that time on the market and getting cozy with the Grinch called DOM. In today's market, it takes about 5 to 7 days for the entire GLOBAL marketplace to notice your property online. If you don't have an offer in two weeks, you're overpriced. Yep, I said it. A lot of "experts" (read: non-experts) will say "but!" or "hey!" at this point. Sorry Bobby, welcome to the reality of the Interwebs. What else if you don't do PPF? You show up late to the party and hit the market not ready, to show the world your (well...it's my) giant digital-and-analog arsenal of marketing genius, all because your house isn't really ready to "have company."

Staging, and Other Unnatural Sightings

Do You Know How Much I Paid for That Couch?

I KNOW, EVERYONE'S TALKING about it ... "Who's your stager?" "Who staged this?" Et cetera, et cetera. OK, very few people outside of real estate think about it... well... unless you're a stager or designer. Guess what? This stuff works, and it works more than well. NAR stats show homes that are professionally staged sell faster and for more money than those homes that aren't staged or are vacant. Who cares about NAR stats? MY stats show it! EVERY TIME! When we talk about this and I say, "Hey, do you want to sell faster and for more money, or slower and net a lot less?" What's probably going to be your answer? But who cares what NAR & I say? I say it! Their stuff sells better than your stuff ... almost every time. (The 'almost' is in the rare case that your stuff is better than their stuff.)

I know your answer already. It's "No! We want to show the property 100 times and be on the market way more than 120 days and eventually sell it for a lot less than you originally told us we could get!" This isn't going to happen, right? You're not going to tell me that. You're going to say, "Faster and for more money, please!" The next couple of subjects might be touchy to a lot of you, so proceed with caution! It's a marketing plan, and here it is: When we talk about a "marketing plan," it's not about you or your house or your taste in decor, your furnishings, your flooring, the orangeish hue of your Formica countertops, your expensive drapes and your lovely choice of wallpaper.

It's part of a PLAN

    Proper

    Logistics

    And

    Nahledge

    PLAN- see it now?

It's a proven plan to sell a property. I understand that "property" happens to be your home, and that "stuff" happens to be your stuff, but we want to sell your house quickly, for the most money and in the shortest amount of time, right? The staging is part of a *plan*, not an *opinion*. It's a *proven plan* to market a home in today's environment. We're not attacking your taste or your decorator Bonachella Nutella III. Got it? It's a **PLAN** to sell a house. When we market a home, who are we marketing it to? Your neighbors? Everyone in Playa Vista? No. We're marketing it to EVERYONE! Read that again ... EVERYONE! We're not marketing it to you. You, the homeowner, are not our target. You're not our buyer. You're trying to get rid of it, remember silly?

We're marketing it to as many potential buyers as possible. How do you present a property to a wide group of people? You make it as generic as possible. Yes, generic, not boring. It needs to appeal to a wide swath of *everyone*.

ge·ner·ic

je'nerik: Pleasing to many; Not generally something you'd like; Also a type of cheap cat food.

Let's see if I can answer some of your questions here.

Design vs. Staging

When I bring stagers in, they're pros. They've done this more than you have even though you frequent Home Goods. They have skills. More skills than your neighbor Bobby, who had a real estate license back in the 80's. Designers design... wallpaper, color schemes, textures, light and plumbing fixtures, etc. And stagers... they have furniture and accessories that are widely loved and coveted today. Key word: *today*. Whatever is hot in our current market environment, they have it. You know, the stuff that's in the magazines that everyone sees but few have, probably even including me and you. When was the last time you bought a couch? A chair? Dining set? See what I mean? Most people out there bought that leather sofa when the kids were one and three. Now, they're 29 and 37. Where does the time go? I'm not saying your taste in furniture or decor is bad, it's just probably not what's currently hot, that's all. If it is, great! I'm still going to bring my stager in for an opinion. And YES... they're decorators... and YES... they have an opinion!

They're way better at this staging thing than you and I. They work with whatever 'design' you have in your house. Remember when I said we need to appeal to the most potential buyers out there? That's why we bring in a pro and we spruce it up into whatever is hot today, and guess what? Remember the stats? They're right ... the voodoo they do actually works! I currently have a house listed, and at first, I showed it vacant and a little dirty to a few buyers. Remember premarketing? When the same buyers saw it after it was staged, every one of them said, "Wow! This house looks totally different than when I saw it before." Some people have trouble picturing where to place furniture. It's a secret science of decorators.

Even the owners came in and said, "Wow! This is a nice house. It looks totally different!" It was their own house, and one they lived in for 20 years. That house sold in a week, after three offers, at full asking price. The seller listened to me. He did what I suggested. Guess what? It worked! It took us almost a month of PPF until we hit the market. When we hit the market, we hit it strong and prepared, and blitzed the Interwebs and our community with it. That's how it's done kids.

If your house is vacant and empty... then YES! It needs to be staged STAT! Most buyers have very little imagination when walking into a vacant property. I get asked... "What room is this?" Me: "Ummm the kitchen... see the range and the sink?" Your property will sell MUCH faster staged than if it's currently vacant.

Fun fact # 37

> The entire industry of staging was created in L.A. in the late 2000's. A cat named Brett Baer was one of the founding fathers as it were. After staging over 1,100 homes worth over $5 billion, he has his own stats. He states in the $2-$5M range, there's no better investment a seller can make because he's averaging an extra 3-5% to the selling price vs. similar homes in the area that are not staged or are stark vacant. This stuff works!

Chapter four recap. PPF stands for:

A. Pandas Playing Football
B. Preachers Praying Fast
C. PrePlanning Fun
D. all of the above

If you chose D, excellent! Go back a few pages and start again. PPF works because we team up with experts to help us present property in its best condition while looking its best for showings. This stuff is *planned*, it doesn't just happen. Most agents you talk to won't even suggest this type of thing because it's a lot of work. It takes asking difficult questions, making difficult decisions, spending a little money up front to make more in the end. My coach, Carl White, taught me to write small checks in order to make big checks, and I pass that infinite wisdom on to my clients.

Read slowly:

Write small checks to make big checks!

CHAPTER 5

Pricing Flotsam and Stratagem - "I'm Not Going to Give it Away" and Other Hilarious Sayings

H ERE'S REAL ESTATE in a Nutshell. Location, Location, Location. Right? Remember that? EVERYONE says that at cocktail parties, communions, chats in the meat department at Vons. The 3 L's!

But when you're selling... it comes down to the REAL Big Three! What? There's another three? Yes!

Price – Condition – Location

That's the Big Three that matter when you're ready to sell. We'll talk about those.

Price- It's all about price! 1- Underprice it for multiple offers 2-Price it at Market and wait and see 3- Overprice it (that's a fancy way of saying that YOU get to pick the price... which will be too high... and thus netting you more DOM and missed showings and doors left open etc. More about those details later.

Condition- What does your house look like? Perfection? Needs some updating? Needs some fixing? Tear down? Of the Big Three… YOU… the seller can change the Price AND the Condition. You can update it, paint it, re-floor it, remodel it, etc. The one thing that you cannot change:

Location- You can't change Location… So Location is still very important because it's the one thing you cannot change. Location affects value. Especially around here! That Ocean… if you're looking at it at home, sitting on your couch… that's going to affect the value for sure! "Sit down views" is a term we use on the coast. When we say "views" we mean Ocean Views. I think you can figure out the sitting down part. Other terms that are HUGE and affect value are: White water views and Sand views. Terms we don't like to use are Power pole views or Sewage Treatment Plant views. More, or less on that later.

So we're going to talk about the Big Three and where you are in the space time continuum regarding those three things. All of them affect what your house is worth.

I've bought and sold a lot of properties in my career and I know firsthand how it feels to be a seller and a buyer. I've been a seller dealing with my own money and profits and my very own personal DOM. I felt all those feelings you feel. I get it. It's nerve-wracking to wait for an offer, wait for a response … to wait for everything. I think I've left money on the table a few times and I feel that maybe I could've gotten a little bit more money from the buyer, but I didn't want to risk it.

I found that by maintaining an "everybody wins" mantra in my life and thus, my real estate business, that life is *way* better! I mean, it's way better! Less stress, less "majoring in the minors". More dealing with the real issues and not sweating the small stuff. I found that when everybody wins, well, everybody wins! If a buyer gets the house and they move in and they're thrilled, then they win. If a seller sells a house at market value and they're happy to have that part out of the way, they win. Everyone, including me, can resume sleeping through the night. It's possible, and it happens a lot. Yeah, being everyone's psychologist is a big part of my job. (In a Freud voice) "So tell me about your mother."

When I first got in the biz, an old guy told me, "Don't stop the parade by bending down to pick up a dime." That changed my whole global value on negotiations. I've never forgotten it. Don't stop forward momentum to over-negotiate, to major in the minors, to get all bunched up over the insignificant. I personally sold my own homes that I wish were worth more than I sold them for. I have not been happy about the current market value of a couple of them. I know how that feels. Yet, market data and trends change and you and I cannot personally change the data because we want more than our house is currently worth. I get it.

"Don't stop the parade by bending down to pick up a dime." -Old guy

It feels like you're getting ripped off. It's a natural thing, this feeling. This feeling of wanting a bit more. We all have it flowing through our veins and it's totally natural. The bigger question is, how do you react if the market isn't where you thought, or where "big data" told you it was? How many times have I heard it? Thousands of times. I get it ... for all of the above reasons. It's still funny to me. "I'm not going to GIVE it away!"

I guess the funny part for me is I'd never ask anyone to give away their house. I mean, that would be quite a thing. If you just gave someone your house, it would be Beach Reporter worthy, maybe even Daily Breeze-esque.

Headline: *Man Gives House Away ... Even Though He Said He Wouldn't!*

Here's the straight talk. There's the value range in your area for houses similar to yours. We should price it here. Do you agree? If not, why? Remember the first questions I'm going to ask you when we meet? Where are you going and how soon do you have to be there? Here's another math equation.

Price Equals Time.

The higher the price, the longer the time it'll take to sell. Likewise, the lower the price, the less DOM to sell. Easy math ... yes? I didn't do well in Geometry either. If you chose the "high" road, here are three things that are likely to happen in regard to time:

1. It'll take time for you to see that you're not getting offers and it's not actually my "faulty marketing plan" that's causing it. It's your faulty pricing strategy that's causing it.
2. It'll take time for the market to come up to your price, say 12-50 years.
3. It'll take time to find a buyer who doesn't care what the price is and just wants your house no matter what, and they'll even give you an extra $100,000 just to make sure you know they're serious. (#3 was a joke answer and not a real one!)

There are strategies to price your property.

1. Price it a bit under market to attract multiple offers ... except remember ... the internet changed everything. You cannot underprice a home anymore without the entire market knowing about it immediately. I'll say it again. You

CANNOT UNDERPRICE A PROPERTY if you put it on the correct channels on the Internet! It's called the World Wide Web for a reason, kids. There's your global marketing. Everyone who's looking for what we've got will see it online immediately with 24/7 reach. If you underprice it. It will sell very quickly and you will probably get multiple offers. Unless it's a crappy market and then it may take a while to find out how low 'underpricing' is. If you don't get any offers in the first 7 days. Then the World Wide Web and all the minions inside of it have spoken. You're OVERPRICED! Period! Remember what I said 10 times already? The internet changed EVERYTHING!

Sorry for all the CAPS ... but I'm trying to get this locked and loaded into your mindset. This is the current reality and if you haven't bought or sold real estate in the last 3 years, this is the Game Changer! Moving on.

2. Price it right at current market.
3. Price it over market for maximum market time. "I'm not going to give it away!" (Cue old guy shaking his fist in the air.)
4. Follow whatever your St. Joseph Home Selling kit(s) buried in the yard tell you to do.

A property isn't a bank account that you can withdraw whatever you want or need out of it. It's worth what it's worth, not what you or Zilly think its worth. (I'll give you a hint here: The answer isn't #3, but it could be #4 under the right circumstances.)

Sometimes there are properties that are more difficult to determine a value for, and then we must "test the market." For instance, a 3,700-square-foot, 1-bedroom home with an ocean view and legal-non-conforming apartment built over the garage on an extra-wide lot. Otherwise ... "testing the market" ... just because you want more money is a bad idea.

Testing the market costs DOM. Yikes! (Picture me running away from **DOM** zombies while looking back over my shoulder in fear.) Plus, it wastes your time, and that of the listing agents and buyer's agents. Remember the Interwebs?

Let's listen to the voice of reason here. But why would reason have anything to do with what people think? Have you read any online reviews? Now that the Sea of Humanity has a "voice"... they do it in online reviews. Hint: The most misspelled words and horrible vernacular wins!

"MY Internet Changed Everything." - Al Gore

Let's talk about selling off market (pocket listing). Who would not want exposure to the MLS? You'd be surprised. I live in the beach cities of Manhattan, Hermosa and Redondo Beach – The South Bay, which is very close to Los Angeles. We have sports stars, TV and movie personalities, big personalities, CEO's, COO's, COW's, millionaires, and billionaires here, and some people have a privacy thing. They don't want you coming over at an open house and nosing around in their closet.

We actually sell houses off market quite often here, because of that privacy thing. People just don't want you in their house. It does happen. Now, if I put a house on the MLS and its then exposed via the internet to every agent out there and all of the buyers who are working with agents and not working with agents, then yes, that would be marketing it to a bigger swath of people. Yet if I have a seller who doesn't want people in their house and they want us to sell it without putting it on MLS and just by networking, then that's what we do. Of course, we'll tell them what I just told you, but it does happen. It's a thing. So is knowing a lot of people named Bobby ... that's a thing, too.

Okay, so you have some background on what you need to think about before moving forward. But wait, you haven't even hired me yet! Exactly how do you sift through the seemingly endless supply of real-A-Ders? In the South Bay, I think every other person has a real estate license. It's hard to meet someone who doesn't know a dozen or 200 agents. So how do you do it? In a sustainable way?

A. Go to the DMV and find one there.
B. Hang out in any bar and they're sitting on both sides of you at any given moment.
C. Read the next chapter.

CHAPTER 6

Selecting An ~~Agent~~ Angel

Happy Hour is Not for Sissies

CUTE STORY: AN agent – let's call him Daryl – walks into a bar. Why, you ask? Well, real estate agents hang out in bars ... a lot. Why, you ask? Well, that's just where we meet other real estate agents and gather to talk about you. Remember the psychologist comment? After long days of real estateing and being an "unlicensed shrink," we have to talk to somebody about whom and what we're dealing with, so we drink. A LOT. We walk into bars and meet other agents and talk about you. We drink water, of course, as well. Bars all over the world are full of real estate agents; just pop your head into Ercoles in downtown Manhattan Beach on any given day. Yup! There you are. Oh wait ... I just happen to be sitting next to you.

I might be down at Fonz's though... that wine list! (Sigh) Now that you're feeling even more encouraged about me and my professional colleagues, I have to answer the obvious question that this chapter was named about. Why do you need an agent? One, you need someone to blame when your house doesn't sell. Two, you need someone to clean your house and toilets for open houses. Three, you really need a cheap psychologist. No! It's not any of those ... keep reading. You need an agent for: representation, guidance, expert knowledge and opinion, up-to-the-minute real-estate market knowledge. You'd also benefit greatly from someone who knows PPF and the average DOM in your area. Practices HTCS and OTB. And while I'm at it, do you know how many pages of disclosure we currently have in California?

"Hire a pro. It costs the same as hiring an idiot."
--Engineer who built the Titanic

Would you perform surgery on yourself? Represent yourself in court? Go by yourself to climb Mt. Everest? Even if you read a book about it, went to a seminar about it, watched a couple of videos on YouTube about it? Even if you sold a house once by yourself, if you haven't sold in the last two years, a lot has changed ... you'd be a danger to yourself. It's tricky business. Making a mistake at this level could cost you tens or even hundreds of thousands of dollars. If a lawsuit ensues, go ahead and triple that number. Yikes! Let's agree to agree here. Hire a pro; not your cousin, your neighbor, friend, guy in the office (Bobby) who has a license ... unless I'm one of those, of course!

Yes, it will cost you money to hire us. SHOCKING NEWS! You know who charges way more? Attorneys ... surgeons ... anesthesiologists ... and you don't tell them they're not worth the money or argue with them about their fees. What if you upset them and they don't do the "best job they can?" Who loses then? You, of course! The same thing goes for the real estate world. Hire a pro. It costs the same as hiring an idiot (see Titanic Architect's memoirs). Life is easier knowing that you have someone playing in your field with you, with your best interests in mind ... not just playing in left field. You need to ask them what kind of things they're going to do to market your property.

HTCS

I call this part of my Marketing Suite: HTCS. Easy, right? Ok... it's

High Touch Concierge Service

I've abandoned the Mega-Team approach for High Touch Concierge Service *HTCS* based on helping you and your needs. In the past, I had multiple team members in my office; I was a big shot... blah blah blah. Now I work smarter and I outsource to pros to do the things I cannot. I don't spend nearly as much time managing a team or getting half-assed results, because I'm using pros outside of my workspace. Its soooo much more efficient and you get a much smoother and delightful experience. Outsourcing pros is waaaaay better than hiring someone to handle the things that come up in transactions and helping my clients figure things out. I have full time pros... all have been doing what they're doing for a long time and are very skilled and very efficient. Therefore, I don't have to stay in the office training staff and then following up to see if they did their job. Would you rather be chatting with Brittany ... who just started at Mega Team SuperStars ... and is 18 and is fairly good at taking messages, or would you rather work with highly trained, self-motivated, able-to-think-on-their-feet sub-contractors compiled by me, a 30-plus year real estate pro to help you get from Pointe A to Pointe B*? (*see reference to France below) I know ... my questions are sometimes so obvious, it's embarrassing.

My team is full of self-starters and better at what they do than I am. That's why you get to talk to me most of the time. Because I'm not managing, I'm doing what I do best. Being with YOU ... and your friends ... and strangers I met at open houses. Which can be weird ... wait ... did we meet at an open house? Disregard last two sentences ... but not this sentence ... the two prior to this one.

#1 thing I've learned:

More Pre-Planning-*PPF* and OTB eliminates stress, problems later, canceled contracts, second and third negotiations, closing delays and nets you MORE Every time!!! I believe in an up front, no nonsense approach to selling real estate. I will be honest with you about pricing and values and you need to promise to do the same. It all comes down to 3 things:

1. Price
2. Location
3. Condition
4. Sustainability*

   *Okay … 4. We are REQUIRED to use the word Sustainability a certain number of times by the Coastal Commission. In a sustainable way, of course (there … I just knocked out 3 more).

*Pre Planning Fun and Outside The Box Thinking

MY High Touch Concierge Service (HTCS) is different from THEIR 'listing checklist'. It's WAAAAY over-the-top service. It's the idea that I want to pre-empt whatever you may encounter and help you get the stuff done easier and faster than you can do it by yourself. We handle things for you when they come up, because you're busy! I want to go so far over the top in the level of service I provide that I show up in your conversations with your friends about how amazing your experience was with me that they and anyone you tell about me and my program, can't wait to talk to me about helping them get from Pointe A to Pointe B. Why do I use the 'e' in Pointe? It's because it automatically looks more expensive and elegant and French-ish. This is just part of my Marketing Suite called PPF, HTCS & OTB. See!?

Listing: What kind of services are offered by your agent? MLS, syndication, worldwide marketing. Ever heard of the World Wide Web? People ask if we market globally ... Zillow, Trulia, Realtor.com, Redfin, Bird Internet and the likes.

Why I'm different. I'm a professional problem solver. A non-stop learner. A social media wizard. A video nutcase and a marketing czar. I practice OTB. Outside the Box creative thinking and creative marketing. Not always doing it like everyone else. OK ... almost NEVER doing it like everyone else. Remember the definition of insanity?

"Doing the same thing over and over and expecting a different result" - Insanity

Photos: Day, night, video tour, VR (virtual reality), drone, 3D imaging, Matterport ... wait, what? SpaceX Falcon 9 flyovers. Having a proper taped/floor plan. Will there be a custom website? Does it work or not work? How can you tell? Do I need a sign out front? Better question, do you really want to sell? Those text-for-info riders are so 2000s. Print ads, flyers and brochures: do they work in today's internety digital world? Baking cookies before an open house to attract buyers is soooo 90s! Baking organic-seed and nut crackers with extra hemp seeds is soooo 21st.

Digital flyers. Guys spinning the arrow sign. Open houses: do they work for you? Mega open house, neighborhood wine-and-cheese party open house. Brokers' open done right, follow-ups, lockboxes versus appointment only. Are they safe? Clowns versus mimes. Are they safe? "My neighbor told me" ... real estate experts versus "a guy on a plane," contract negotiation. What bar (bars) do you typically hang out in? Getting along with others while moving things along

... lemon versus sugar. Timeline management. Proper technique for making S'mores. Soooooo many details!

Maybe you're beginning to understand that the most important part of all of this is to have others who help handle those things because really, who has time for all this stuff? Listen kids, this is a FULL-TIME JOB! Yes, a real J-O-B. If you want to hire your pal Bobby in account management because he also has a real estate license and he's told you 100 times he can help you sell your house (in his spare time), well ... go back and start at the beginning of this book and stop looking at your phone. . Really! Bobby is a terrible idea for you. He doesn't have the time, skill, market knowledge or enough contract knowledge to help you cook on the barbecue. Don't hire "part-time Bobby" to help you sell or buy real estate. It won't work out well for you.

There are so many others on my team, each of them experts in their own area: Home inspectors, handymen, painters, stagers, designers, house cleaners, photographers, drone photographers, videographers, custom sign creators, custom sign riders, office support staff, paperwork doers and inputters, bulky mailers, media managers, middle managers, social media posters, advertising designers, clowns, video editors, planners, caterers, mimes, wine shop owners, cheese mongers, custom printers, postcard writers, pushy Girl Scout cookie salespeople, inviters, flyers, mailers, acronym maker-uppers and that's not even a complete list!

Ask, ask, ask about a real estate agent's marketing plan before you hire them. Most agents in the beach cities have a very complicated marketing plan. I'll share it with you even though it's a revered secret among this large group of agents. Remember, it's EXTREMELY complicated. It has lots and lots moving parts. It's called the "South Bay Lazy Agent Marketing Plan."(SBLAMP) It goes like this:

1. Let the seller choose any price they want regardless of the comps because I NEED a listing
2. Wednesday, sign up in the yard. Exciting!
3. MLS on Thursday. Exciting!
4. Brokers' open Thursday or Friday, depending on the city. Earth shattering!
5. Public open house Saturday and Sunday, 2-4 p.m. BORING! (Because 12-4 is twice as many hours they have to work, and who has time to do that?)
6. Review offers on Wednesday

And Thursday rolls around and ... NO OFFERS! Hmm, that's it. The SBLAMP! (South Bay Lazy Agent Marketing Plan)

Then they say, "Something must have gone wrong. Let's start over. Let's do another brokers' open, just in case." Open house Saturday and Sunday from 2-4 p.m., review offers on Wednesday. Thursday the next week comes and again no offers. They say, "But I spent four hours this weekend working. I'm exhausted!" Meanwhile, you know what creeps up? Yep! DOM ... tick, tick ... Then you've had the listing almost as long as you've had that leather couch. This "lazy agent plan" is most certainly "part" of a marketing plan, but it shouldn't be THE ENTIRE marketing plan. If it is, don't hire them. Call me!

Remember PPF? Plan, write small checks to make big checks, sell faster, net more, easier closing with less stress. Which sounds better to you? Moving forward. At this point I'm ready to put your property live on MLS, everything up to then has been PPF (Pre-Planning Fun, remember?) MLS is live, and then there's the neighbors' wine and cheese open house, the brokers' open house, and the public open houses. A lot of marketing has gone into my listings before they hit the MLS, as you could see in the above lists. Then, we're working the websites. We're working the social media sites, boosting posts, running ads either via social media or print or skywriting, which I'll cover thoroughly in the next chapter.

We're doing a lot of follow up to get a contract and preferably multiple contracts. When we get a contract, we ask if any of the other interested parties want to jump in as well. We want multiple contracts because that will help my seller – you – get a better offer with less moving parts. We negotiate a fair offer and it gets accepted. Once we're under contract with the buyer, my transaction team steps in to handle every detail, all 4.5 million of them. Escrow team? Yes, this team matters. There are some terrible escrow teams out there, yikes! The title team checks your title to make sure that it's clear and clean.

By the way, we check escrow and title when I start PPF, because if you've got a cloud on your title, sometimes it takes time to get that stuff removed. We first check the title and make sure it's squeaky clean. If not, we have time to work on it. Back to my ever-growing list of contributors: Handymen and tradespeople. A termite and pest team. A home warranty team. Don't laugh ... this team can save you thousands of dollars just because the rep wants my business. Professional movers can literally make it easy or terrible to move. Do I have a great moving company? Of course I do. House cleaners, again. Then, after marketing, wait! What's that?

Now that we're here. You and me. I can tell you that this ENTIRE BOOK is my marketing plan! Compare this 14 chapter book about PPF and DOM and tons of humorous anecdotes with their "marketing checklist" they pulled off the internet. Who would you rather work with? "Famous" Best Selling Author* or someone who has the internet and access to a printer? Did I mention I'm glad you're here?

*In my own mind

There are so many moving parts to a marketing plan and every house can be a little different. I'm always adding valuable pieces to my plan as they occur to me or as they're introduced to the market. Technology is changing the way we market every month, it seems. There's always something new out there: Software, hardware, drones, phones, cameras, apps, robots, weirdly shaped hammers. One more thing: If you're reading this 10 years after I publish this, our current marketing plan is to tell the robots to go and find a buyer and they do it. If you're reading this 20 years after I publish this, there won't be any more houses because all the robots have killed us and ruined the earth. WHY are we building robots? Didn't you see The Matrix?

Low-Balls and Multiples ... Getting an Offer and Counter-Offer / Counter-Terrorism

I CURRENTLY HAVE A house under contract that we had multiple offers on. Great! Another agent called me – let's call her Bobbi – to ask if she could write an offer and I said, no way! Wait ... I did not say that. I told her what the offers were and told her to meet or beat them. The next day, she sent me an offer for $200,000 below list price. My two other offers were at list price and above list price, which I had told her the previous day.

Needless to say, her buyer didn't get the house. Whoops! She told me her buyer wanted to "test the market." This happens a lot, and it's based on a few things. One, most commonly, you're new to the marketplace, you don't have a clear grasp of what's happening here in the market. You do what your father taught you to do, you LOW-BALL them. You start really low and you go up slowly, right? Act like you're not interested. Who doesn't know someone with that philosophy? However, if you're in a strong seller's market or a runaway seller's market, there is NO WAY you'll ever buy a house if you maintain that outdated maxim.

If you've ever been a buyer in that market, you know what I'm talking about. Picture this: You walk into my open house. You're new to the area, or you're new to buying a house. You like the house and you ask me to help you write an offer. I tell you what's going on in the marketplace currently, that it's strong. I also tell you that you're not going to like what I say to you next. You say, "Go ahead." Then I tell you that there are already two offers on the house and one is $100,000 over the list price. You laugh at me because EVERYONE tells you to LOW-BALL all the time!

After you write five offers on five different properties and get zero accepted, you start to see that you're in a hot market and I actually was telling you the truth the first day. I was trying to help you that first day, but you had to learn yourself because EVERYONE tells you to NEVER trust a real estate agent. Whoops! From there, you (hopefully) learn that if you see something, you write your best offer first and fast. Yet, that only took four to five weeks to get you to that point. Trust me ... it's difficult to have that conversation with people. When you're looking at me sideways and thinking, "Hey, that sounds like you're trying to sell me something fast and make me overpay. My dad taught me to low-ball everything. You know ... negotiate! Act like you're not interested."

Now, if it's a strong buyer's market, it's opposite day. Buyers low-ball. They wait for DOM to crank up and make their best deal. I have lots of experience in these markets and I know how to strategize your position. It's a whole other world! Let's say we're in a buyer's market, which means not a lot of buyers are buying. Remember 2008-11? DOM are high everywhere and you have to keep dropping your price until you find what the buyers are willing to pay. A market like that is frustrating and grueling. If we're in that market, none of the following applies.

"Don't Be G-ee!" Bonzo Gibb –
The BeGees Cover Marching Band

As I write this, we are currently in a healthy seller's market or a strong seller's market. That means that homes that are priced right for their location and condition are selling pretty quickly. If you price it right, or underprice, you could get multiple offers. These conditions, however, have been known to cause a person to become Greedy. I call it the "G-Factor" or G-Facto for short. It can cloud your ability to be logical about what's going on. I had sellers – let's call them Bobby and Diane – who wanted $2 million for their house. The market was pretty strong at the time.

I told them they could probably get a bit more than that and suggested we put it on the market at $2 million and see if we get multiple offers. We did ... only because I was wearing my lucky flip flops, right? Well, we got more than $2.1 million and then the G-Factor kicked in. Instead of being giddy, they became G-ee and wanted to raise the price. Wait, what? They wanted $2 million; I got an offer higher than that. Now you want me to tell those buyers to go away and raise the price and piss everyone off who's given you an offer and perhaps get involved in a lovely lawsuit? Excellent theory, Mr. Watson!

I'm just saying ... money can cause people to hop on the weird-express-train to G-Facto in a fast hurry and mess up everything. Keep a sharp eye out for the G train. Remember, "Don't stop the parade to bend over and pick up a dime." Greed ... can make you crazy! Don't be G-ee!

Multiple offers or low-balls, what to expect? It's a funny thing ... **DOM** ... We do our PPF ... We underprice or price it on the money ... on purpose. We premarket like a boss ... we had buzz going about the house before it's even on the market ... maybe even a few pre-showings. We get the house staged. We have a professional photographer making it look very sexy. I'm not shooting pictures with my iPhone any more. Nor am I buying as much jewelry on HSN as I used to. BTW, one of those last two sentences was not true.

Then, we go live on MLS and what if we get an offer – or more – the first week? Well, we did all of the above and we priced it correctly and now we have an offer. You should be mad, right? Upset because you didn't get to clean your home 270 times for 119 showings, 48 of which were no-shows? You want to savor a lazy 234 **Days On Market.** You want to enjoy keeping the house clean and having multiple parties of strangers with dirty shoes and unattended children in your house for nine months. You love having all the lights on or half the doors open when you arrive home, or getting locked out of the garage because you didn't heed my advice to hide a key in the garage. Right?

No silly! You're not mad, you're giddy, remember? Excited! Someone wants to buy your house today. Take the following quiz.

Chapter Seven quiz: We priced your home correctly and now we have multiple offers. Now what?

> A. Be mad you weren't allowed months on the market with multiple showings and no shows and doors left open and open house after open house without an offer.

> B. Be happy you hired a pro who uses weird acronyms and makes up words.

Hint: It's not A. How did you do on the quiz? Hopefully you chose B. No? Okay, we have work to do.

Let's look at the buyers and their agents, who to counter and how to counter. We look at the buyer. How strong are their financials? Will they pay in cash or finance? How much cash down? What is the contingency period? When is close of escrow? (We call that COE.) Do we know the agent? What's their reputation like? How about their attitude? Are they an over-negotiator? Are they problem children? Will they be easy to work with, or non-stop problematic? Based on all that information, we counter the strongest buyers our terms, then we tell them to produce the highest and best offer and see what we get.

BEWARE ... The Letter

Those Buyers ... they wrote me a letter ...

If there's a real pro agent representing the buyer, then there's The Letter! The letter the buyer sends you with their offer ... it's an introduction to who they are. A person, a couple, a family, a cute pack of coyotes ... with pictures and a paragraph on the back of each one, explaining who they are and why they want your house and why you should accept their offer. Exercise extreme caution! This will be a gushy letter about the family with pictures of cute puppies and sometimes kids. Now this is an EXTREME ninja tactic that WE will use when you're a buyer working with me. This is a way to make a buyer look stronger in the eyes of the seller. Yes! You're the seller! How does it work? Remember the term 'Sex Sells'? This has nothing to do with that! This tactic, however, is meant to sway you over to them via the super power called 'emotion.' "Look at my cute kids or cute cat videos or my uncle Bob in a clown outfit. See? I have a cute ferret rescue service... or cute snakes...", whichever fits. "We'll take good care of your house and fondly tell the stories of how this was previously a 'meth house,' and how the old neighbor Bobby wandered off after falling off the ladder on Columbus Day." You get the picture ... it's a GREAT tactic to help you stand out if you're a buyer competing with other offers. If you're a seller, however, and susceptible to highly charged emotional moments, or if you're a tough guy and don't want anyone seeing you cry, then this could be rough for you as a seller when confronted with "The Letter". You've been warned! As your agent, I will ask you if you want to see "The Letter". If not, then maybe you can be more neutral. Everyone's different. So I ask.

Backup offers, should I or shouldn't I? Most buyers agents don't want to tie up their buyer into a backup offer if the buyer is actively looking for a house. They want to keep moving and keep options open in case something perfect comes up the next day. It's a tough call for them. As a seller though, if I can get a backup offer, we always take one because it keeps buyer No. 1 on track. If buyer No. 1 knows another potential buyer is breathing down their neck wanting them to bail out, it will keep them motivated to close early, or at least on time.

How about a buyer with a sale contingency versus a close-of-escrow contingency? What does that mean? Let's say you own a house in the Manhattan Beach Tree Section and you want to move closer to the beach. You don't like that one mile to the beach. You want to be three blocks. You put your house on the market and we go down to the beach and we find a house that's perfect for you, and you want to write an offer on it. If we wrote an offer and you need the proceeds from your house in the Manhattan Beach Tree Section to buy the house in the Hermosa Beach Sand Section, that would be a contingency sale. We would write an offer. If the seller agreed, we would say, "We want to buy your house, but we are going to make it contingent upon us finding a buyer AND selling AND closing escrow on our house in the Tree Section." If the seller says okay, he's tying up his house with a question mark for an unknown timeframe. We don't know when we can close on the new house because you're waiting for a buyer on yours.

It's a bit MORE complicated than that, but I'm trying to keep it simple. Most sellers will not agree to contingency sales in a strong market. If you are in a buyer's market, sellers will be more open to that.

Let's say that you have an offer on your house in the MB Tree Section, now we can go to that house in the HB Sand Section and write an offer just contingent upon the close of escrow of your house. We have a time frame then because you know that your buyer is going to close in 30 days on yours and you want to close in 35 days on the new one. You can show them it's still contingent upon your buyers performing in a timely fashion but there is a timeframe and you actually have a buyer.

More sellers would be more interested in THIS kind of thing more than the first example. Does that make sense?

Moving on. Successful low-balling depends upon what kind of market you're in. I've always had the philosophy to counter every offer; unless it's full price and cash (we accept those!) Counter the low ones also, because it could be their dad talking, or the guy on the plane talking, or the weird neighbor and real estate non-expert Bobby talking. What if they came up to your price and accepted it? You don't know if you don't ask. If I get a low ball, I will counter. In a sustainable way. In a Buyer's market, a "Low Ball' offer *maybe* at actual market value and you will need to look hard at these offers! Especially if prices are falling!

Are we having fun yet?

CHAPTER 8

Inspections and Contingency Periods – Yes, Real Math

Calendaring For Fun and Profit!

O UR CONTRACT DEFAULT days for inspections are 17 days for inspections and 21 days for financing contingencies to be removed. That means just that: The buyer has those calendar days to remove those contingencies. If it's a strong seller's market, we can usually shorten those timeframes. (We are currently doing it 7-10 days for inspections and 14 days for financing.) Sometimes smart buyers whittle down those timeframes in a hot seller's market in order to make their deal more appealing and get their offer accepted.

There have been times the buyers are very certain they will get financing, so they will come in with no financing contingencies whatsoever. That's a strong play and you have to be a very, very strong buyer to do that ... and very experienced because that is not for the faint of heart. If you're putting down 3 percent earnest deposit and can't get a loan for whatever reason, and there were no financing contingencies, your earnest deposit – which could be $100,000 depending on the price of the home – could be subject to forfeiture. That's an expensive thing to have happen.

The loan contingency period is 21 days or less. If the loan isn't approved at the end of that contingency, now what? You, as a seller, have options. You could:

A. Give the buyer a three-day notice to remove the contingency and prove that they have their loan. (They'll forfeit their earnest deposit if they do not close.) If after three days they don't remove their contingency, you can cancel the contract and escrow.

B. You could give them a little more time to remove that contingency or you could just

C. Keep letting them float and see how it goes (I don't recommend C) or

D. Let's just meet at Pancho's and have a margarita

As far as online lenders go, Slowwwen, et al, isn't so quick. If you're a rate shopper and see internet companies and the rates that they're quoting that are so much lower than what the real rates are. It's always a bait and switch scheme. "Oh, we made a mistake!" If those rates quoted look too good to be true… Guess what? I repeat: Those rates are probably *not real*. If they are, you will not be able to get a loan from them because they can't close. They have so many rules about it on purpose. You've got to love robots: "Please press 7 for a lame-ass robot recording. Thank you." Internet lenders are robots. There are people that work there (we've heard … but no one has ever seen one of these people) but instead, you're dialing a 1-800 number with a 15-digit extension. You don't know what country these people are in. You don't know how long they've been doing this. You don't even know if they're dressed!

The service is generally very terrible and very slow. If you need to try to get a hold of somebody – an actual *human* – it's very, very difficult. Who are these people really and where are they? I cannot make a LARGE enough point here. These internet lenders are Terrible in just about every phase of a loan. I have yet to have one turn out amazing! (If you had one that worked out, good for you! Please don't write me a letter to tell me about it #BuyALotteryTicket)

That takes us to local lenders versus non-local lenders, and walking into your bank and asking for a loan. If you have a banking relationship with a lot of cash in the bank, then you would probably want to talk to your bank or your financial planner-type people. They might have a product that would work for you. If not, then I like to work with local pros. Local pros have a local reputation they need to protect. You get this all the time: "A lender promised to do _____ and it's not done, now what?" By the way, there's also an appraisal contingency in our contract. That means that the contract is subject to and contingent upon the home appraising for the purchase price or greater. If the appraisal comes in under the purchase price, that means that that is the highest number that the bank will lend on, minus the down payment. That would mean you would have to change the purchase price downward if that happened, or you would cancel the contract if buyer AND seller didn't agree to this change in value. All the while adding onto DOM. Tick...tick...tick... Remind me ... How soon do you have to be there again?

That whisks us to appraisals and appraisers. They are more fun than you can imagine. What do appraisers really know?

When an appraiser walks up to me and they're appraising your house that's in escrow, I meet them with a contract and copies of the recent comparable sales, the stuff that I showed you way back when we were talking about our PPF, updated to-the-minute by the way. I hand it to them and I show them all of the things you have done to this house. I give them a list of all of the upgrades and blah, blah, blah, and some sort of a dialog about the other houses on the list. I've seen them all.

An appraiser sees the price on the contract and that's the number they're shooting for.

Remember what I told you earlier about my client who had the recent refi appraisal for $2.8 million, and we sold that property for $2.4 million? Only two months had gone by between the refi appraisal and me putting it on the market and that market did not drop during that time. In fact, it was going up! Say what? That appraiser was $400,000 MORE THAN what that property was actually worth? That's almost 20 percent over real market value! Now, tell me. Do appraisers know market value? No, most don't. If they're doing a refi appraisal, they don't have a number to hit. If I'm giving a contract to the appraiser for a purchase appraisal, he knows a price to hit. The Purchase Price. This is what bugs me about appraisers. Everyone is like, "Oh, they're the experts!"

They are not experts. They look in a rear-view mirror, so they're more like historians. They only use data that has already happened. They do not take into account what is happening currently. So if there's a sudden spike in values and the inventory dries up, this will make buyers climb over each other to get a house. This activity drives up prices. Remember in college that stupid course you took ... Econ 101? The boring prof was blathering about 'supply and demand.' Well this is that. This type of market makes appraisers weak in the knees. Because most of them have NO IDEA about values. They just try to aim at a purchase price that's written on an offer. But they're looking at PAST sales ... and the ones in the past are lower ... because we're seeing a spike. So the appraisal comes in low... because the appraisers aren't taking into account multiple offers and no inventory and high buyer demand. PLUS ... appraisers are afraid of underwriters and having to go back and update their appraisal, so they go easy on values (see Chapter 12). Ohhh it's such a fun game to play!

"It's like the cab line in LAX. Whoever's up next ..."

Out-of-area appraisers are lots of fun, too! There's a thing called the HVCC that Frank/Dodd installed after the Mortgage Meltdown in 2008, and that's a round-robin appraisal process which means the good appraisers get punished and the bad appraisers stay in business, much like the cab line at LAX. Whoever's up next ... and woe to your stomach if you get the crappy driver who's driving a friend's cab and you just realized they cannot drive or speak English. Same with an out-of-area appraiser. These guys are licensed! By the State AND Nationally! Again, like someone who works at the DMV and are terrible at their job, they can't get fired. So now you know what can happen when they only use data that has already happened. They do not and cannot take into account what is happening currently. When I walk into your house and you tell me you have a refi appraisal for _____ and I tell you I don't care, now, you know why. But I actually DO care ... deep down! I DO want to see that appraisal ... for one reason: Is the square footage more than the tax assessor shows? If it is, we'll use the appraiser's square footage. Why, you ask? If we're selling at $1,000 per square foot and we now have more square footage to sell ... and if I'm representing you and trying my darndest to get you top dollar. WWDD? (What Would Daryl Do?)

Again ... I have a couple of local appraiser friends who are rock stars! They absolutely know what's going on around here and are my go-tos when I need help figuring out how to price a difficult property. This is not the norm though.

Inspectus Detectus: The Home Inspection

Let's talk about the breakdown with home inspections and repair requests. Remember we talked about PPF? (Pre Planning Fun) We do a pre-inspection, fix the big stuff, and avoid that *Second*

Negotiation. This is where it happens. The LONG repair request list. The buyer thinks the house is going to fall down tomorrow because they look at 42 items on that list and think, "Wow! This house is terrible! Fix everything. We want everything fixed!"

That's generally how the buyers feel. Buyer's request for repairs = *Second Negotiation.* The seller thinks, I'll do this and this, but the buyer is panicking and that can equal a canceled deal. Who is going to pay for termite inspections and repairs? Oh, that's right. We did a termite inspection when we were doing home inspection, so we already know if you have termites. PPF baby! And you have a 90-105 percent chance of having termites!

That's already a given, but not if you didn't pre-inspect! You could have a lot of termite damage around here because we not only have subterranean termites, we have flying termites. Those guys are the worst, because they can just go everywhere all the time. When you see the circus tent covering a house, that's where those flying termites are getting gassed. Do NOT enter said circus tent, btw … it'll be waaaay worse than a real circus! Well… a bit worse. You'll just die of poisoning rather than boredom.

Fun Fact #47:

If your house was "Clear" of termites last month, they could be there today! #WeHateTermites

Sewer-line inspections with a camera, say what? There's a blockage, canceled deal.

Roof inspections and cracked roof tiles. This is how it goes with roof tiles. The guys will go up to check the roof, but they may crack roof tiles while they're on the roof checking the roof tiles … for cracks.

Then they say, "Oh there's cracked roof tiles." Then, the guys go up to tent the house for fumigation, get on the roof and crack more roof tiles. Then, the roofer goes up to replace the cracked roof tiles and he breaks 10 more while walking on the roof tiles, replacing the cracked roof tiles. Cracking roof tiles is fun. If you're like me ... this paragraph really cracked you up.

What about pool and spa inspections? Who has a pool so close to the ocean? Right?

City reports? What???

Do retrofit laws have any teeth? Retrofit what???

And then there are zoning laws: Old versus new and grandfathered versus illegal. How about that addition on the back or the apartment that was built over the garage? How about legal non-conforming? How about that? When I say 'legal non-conforming,' I use it to show you how damn complicated this can be. And yes, 'grandfathered' is a thing. Think about it this way: Your grandfather is farting in the chair over there at Thanksgiving and no one seems to notice or mind, because he's your grandfather. That's what that word means. It's not currently legal, but it's been there farting in the chair so long, no one is currently old enough to remember if it's ok or not, so we let it go. There, does that help? RE: Legal non-conforming, think of it like this ... its 'legal'... but it's also 'non-conforming.' So don't make a fuss if he's farting in the chair over there, ok? Sorry I just used so much legal fart jargon.

Disclosures. Do you have any idea how many pages of disclosures we have in California? (Hint: it's A LOT!) How much do you disclose?

Do you know the difference between mediation and arbitration?

Do you know about the Law Of Attraction? Escrow and escrow instructions? Are you aware that wire fraud is very prevalent right now? And so is wire-tapping and tap-dancing. Another chapter for that though.

Who are title companies and what do they do? Clouds on title. Will it actually rain on my title? Tax liens and other fun things recorded against your property.

NHD, you know what that means, right? How about SPQ, TDS, and AVID?

What cities have transfer taxes? How much? Who normally pays? UGH... this chapter is so BORING!

Who pays that guy on the corner spinning those signs and how do you find them to hire them?

www.GuyOnTheCornerSpinningSigns.com?

Earthquake insurance. Earthquake insurance for condos and townhomes. Are you *really* covered?

You know how to prorate taxes, right? When are they due? When are they late? Supplemental tax... wha?

I ask these silly, difficult, annoying questions only to make a point. Who the heck knows all this stuff and is it ok to make fun of them at parties? Is it ok to even GO to a party after discussing any of this? Remember I said it'll take a while to get your property on the market if we do it correctly?

Disclosurementationism (Latin: Disclosurem Maximus)

Latin is a dead language; it's very plain to see.
It killed off all the Romans, and now it's killing me!

D ISCLOSUREMENTATIONISM IS FUN. In the olden days of yesteryear, like back in the '80s, we had two-page contracts. Yep! That's it! Zero disclosures. ZERO. No inspections other than initial showing and the final walkthrough. We would then turn on the dishwasher, flush the toilets and run all the faucets and hope everything was in the same condition as when we first saw it. The landscape was called "Buyer Beware!" Really, that's what the mentality was in real estate in the '80s. Needless to say, a lot has changed. Mostly there is way less hair. I did have a rocking mustache back then (heavy sigh).

Imagine this. You just closed on your new house and you move in and you're happy, happy, happy. Your doorbell rings. You answer it. It's your next-door neighbor, Bobby (who else?). He welcomes you to the neighborhood, tells you how great all the neighbors are, tells you how glad everyone is that a nice family moved in. He's talking about you and your family there, right? Then he goes on to tell you how everyone's so glad the people who lived in your house moved away and how everyone was sick of the smell of the meth cooking in the house and all the comings and goings of unseemly characters. You stop Bobby right there and you say,

"Wait a minute; you're talking about this house? It was a meth house?"

Bobby says, "Yes. Can't you tell from all the burned wallpaper in the kitchen, and the smell?" You hastily thank Bobby for stopping by, yell out to your family to grab whatever they can and get in the car and you make one call. Who do you call? Either your real estate agent or your attorney. Well, one of those will be thrilled that you called and the other will be the opposite of that. (Hint: The attorney will be thrilled.)

That is a true story. How would you feel if that were you? I mean, really? This has happened more times than anyone can remember. Pre-disclosures and post, it still happens. People choose not to disclose "difficult situations" because they're, well, difficult.

You say to yourself: "Let's just not say anything about it and no one will notice," right? Until neighbor Bobby shows up to your door about five-and-a-half seconds after the moving van left the house. That happens enough times and ta-da! A disclosure is born.

Ok... I can't go on... even *I'm* bored! – The Author

How many pages? How many forms? Here's a list of disclosures we're currently using. If you're like me, skip to the end of this list and continue the riveting rhetoric.

1. Agency
2. NHD
3. AVID

4. Drought
5. Wire fraud
6. Toilet retrofit
7. Building report

Okay, I can't go on ... even I'm bored.

Let's look at the last deal I closed, last week. FYI, by the time you're reading this, it wasn't last week. There were 21 separate disclosure documents – TWENTY-ONE! – totaling 78 pages. Holy crap! And growing ... it seems like we add another disclosure every few months. All brought about by lawsuits no doubt. I can hear it now.

Problem Buyer: "But nobody disclosed that it gets dark here every night and I can't see the ocean."

Daryl: "Please sign this 'It Gets Dark Here Every Night' disclosure."

I get that there's a lot to disclose. As a seller, you need to disclose everything that might affect the value of the house. Somewhere in our universe there has to be some kind of responsibility for having some tiny shards of common sense. Why do we have to DISCLOSE that if you pour hot coffee on your lap, you'll burn yourself? 78 extra pages baby!

It Killed Off All The Romans ...
And Now It's Killing Me

In light of all that depressing thought on the previous page... I'm going to ask you to think hard and remember back in the history of you and your house to remember all the work you've done. All the repairs and updates, and who you hired to do them. Licensed contractors or unlicensed? Did you pull permits? Hire an architect? Did you have plans drawn? What kind of leaks happened over time and where were they? How long ago? What did you do to fix them? If you fixed them, did you get rid of the water stains? That kind of stuff. Remember, you have to be steps ahead of your neighbor Bobby, and list all of the things that might come up after you sell the house. We're still talking about things that may affect the value of the property.

You'll need to write it down in advance. When we get a buyer, we give them all the disclosures and let them look at them to make their own determination on whether they need to further investigate or can move forward. We want to give them everything at the start of the transaction at the inspection period and let them do all the due diligence work up-front. If they're spooked now about something, they can leave peacefully. We do not want them to discover, after they own the house, that you had a guy over to fix the ceiling that caved in from a water leak. He did a hack-job repair on said ceiling and the ceiling caved in…again.

Again, you're going to be shocked when I mention that we don't want that.

We have disclosure forms you fill out. You need to remember all the stuff about the house that went wrong, stuff the neighbor remembers like when the ceiling caved in twice after those rainstorms, and will immediately tell the new buyer when they're moving in their piano upstairs. Too much? Yes. Please don't talk about every crack in the sidewalk. Don't major in the minors. But do mention if there are large aggressive packs of Girl Scout cookie sellers on the block!

Chapter Nine recap.

What should you disclose?

    A. Small cracks in the sidewalk

B. Scratch on the floor

C. sticky door lock

D. Zuul, the gatekeeper of Gozer who is a demigod and minion of Gozer, lives inside your built-in Viking refrigerator and the fridge is included...as-is!

CHAPTER 10

Removing Contingencies and Other Sleight of Hand

D O I REALLY have to remember all this? When the inspection contingency is up, the buyer must remove the contingency in writing, and the same goes for a loan contingency. Inspection contingency is usually shorter than its loan counterpart: 17 days is preprinted in our purchase contract, though it's currently negotiated to 7-10 days. What if they need more time? They can ask for it, and as a seller, you can approve the extra time or say, "Get on with it or cancel." The loan contingency is 21 days pre-printed in our contract. Like I said before, it's usually negotiated around 14 days. Then there's the appraisal contingency, which hinges on the loan contingency, or vice versa, and requires the appraisal to come in at least the purchase price or higher.

If the appraisal comes in lower, there are options, but they're not pretty. What we have done in the past is contested those low appraisals if they did not use correct comps. Wait ... comps? What's that?

Computers? Composygnathus? (That's an ocean-dwelling dinosaur. ... No, it isn't, I made it up, but it sounds like it could be one, right? You've probably never heard of it because no one could remember how to spell it to look it up and see if it was or wasn't a 'disputed dinosaur.') No, silly … Comps = Comparable Sales! We're looking at comparable properties that have sold in the last 90 days (AKA: comps - see what we did there?) and we give the appraiser correct comps and sometimes we have gotten appraisals changed. This doesn't happen as often as it used to in the olden days, though. Ahhh the olden days. I do (not) miss S'mores around a campfire!

This is why you hire me to handle your sale for you. We know the drop dead dates… as opposed to the 'drop dead gorgeous dates'… that's another chapter. We're watching the clock and doing our best to get everyone to take less smoke breaks and handle our stuff in OUR timeline. Me and my Transaction Management Team are keeping an eye out for possible delays and problems and trying to solve them before they come up… You're busy. You've got things to do. Imagine if you were a For Sale By Owner. *FSBO, and you were handling all this on your own without knowing any of the traps and snares I've mentioned so far. Would YOU want to do this on your own with no road map? No… there aren't any road maps. Maybe a stupid infographic you can pull off the internet. "Steps to selling your home". Good luck! While being ushered into that Viking refrigerator that Zuul happens to be living in. Remember? Selling and closing a house is HARD!

Now this is getting better! When the buyer removes all the contingencies, it's time to get ready to close. This deal has a super-high chance of closing. Wait … did I just say "super-high chance" rather than "guaranteed to close?" Well ……………

CHAPTER 11

LOs, aka Loan Officers

But Officer … Do You Want to Play LOL?

I'M NOT SURE where they got the "officer" status but that's what we call them. Fun title, yes? I want to use it!

Me: "Hello ... I'm Daryl ... I'll be your real estate agent officer. You can call me Officer. I'll be handling your transaction very carefully because of my title."

You: "Thank you, Officer Daryl."

Me: "It's just, 'Officer.'"

Loan officers (AKA: LO's) have a lot of pressure on them. What time to get to the office, what time to go to coffee, what time is lunch, what time is tee time, you know ... busy, busy, busy. We're not sure what they *really* do other than the above daily schedule. There are more people working at the mortgage company than you can imagine. LO's, processers, assistants, underwriters, pencil sharpeners, appraisers, closers, coffee runners, document preparers, quality controllers, lobby clowns and more.

There is also a plethora of management above the LO'S who all wear suits (Overdressus Maximus**) and mill about shouting coffee-run orders and such. First ... I need to get on the intercom: *loud feedback noise over speakers* "Attention You Suits and all Wig Salesmen! This is a public service announcement. Stop overdressing! We can spot you a mile away! You and lawyayers, come on guys. Look around. We live at the beach. It's SoCal. It's warm here most of the time. We wear shorts a lot, and flip-flops. Why? Because we can, and this is what our clients are wearing. . You're not fooling anyone with the suit! It's different here, lighten up a bit ... you'll get more people asking you over for Thanksgiving with farting Grandpa." End of public service announcement.

**There seems to be a lot of Latin around here! Whatus Giveus?*

Let's take an in-depth look at a mortgage loan officer, or LO. They'll talk to the buyer on the phone and get details, pull the buyer's credit; they'll run everything through software to get a pre-qualification, or pre-qual. Then, they'll ask the buyer to go to their website and fill out a loan application. Then, they'll send an auto-e-mail asking you for documentation to show that what you wrote in your loan app jives with what really is the case in your real life.

This documentation includes tax returns, every bank statement you've had since college, copies of high school transcripts, your ID, ID statements, statements about the ID statement, photos of your kids and dog, and the jar you keep all your loose change in, to name a few.

This is all pretty typical stuff; it's how they do it that bugs me. It seems like when you're there ... right after you get a pre-qual, you feel great ... like you're going to buy that house ... and then ... unbeknownst to you ... you get stuck. It feels as though maybe this was the first loan they've ever done with a human, and that the whole process is so convoluted and dysfunctional. From that point on; until you get the keys to the house. They already know what documentation they're going to need for you if they've done this at least one time before, but they actually don't ask for everything upfront. They'll wear you down over the next three to four weeks, asking every 10-15 minutes for some other thing.

A copy of that paper napkin you wrote notes on in a bar two years ago. A copy of your paycheck from your first job working at McDonald's in 1987, over and over, the silliest "documentation" so they can find a way to deny your loan application 25 days after they gave you a pre-approval. This is the definition of insanity. Every day ... every loan ... it's like they can't remember the last loan they did last week. They can't figure out where their internal problems are and figure out how to fix them so they can deliver a smoother, more enjoyable, perhaps even more professional experience to buyers everywhere. Nope. Every loan is a struggle. It's archaic and clunky. Maddening is another word that pops into my head. F#*%&!_#^!d up is another word picture that pops into my head as well but I'm not going to tell you what that crazy first word was at the beginning of this sentence. (I know you just glanced back to see what it might be)

It's like when your mom always invited your annoying drunk lawyayer uncle over for Thanksgiving year after year even though he ruined the event every year. It just makes no sense.

That said, there ARE a handful of LO's who HAVE figured this out and can deliver a professional experience to our clients, but it's a very small list. My mentors Carl White and Scott Hudspeth, who are AMAZING Loan Originators! Not only do they "get it" and know how to make this process easy and smooth and enjoyable ... they help other LOs in the US to 'see the light' and start solving these perennial issues before they happen and make this experience YELP-Y (in a good way). I love those guys BTW. They've taught me a ton and I owe them a lot! I only want to work with people like them for obvious reasons. Hint: It's not ALWAYS the company you saw on the internet with the best rates. Also, just as all LO's are not the same, all real estate agents are not the same. If you're here, you already know this. (HINT: Daryl is NOT the same as other agents.)

Let's play a game. It's called

LOL: Loan Officer Lingo

What they say = What they meant

No problem = Problem.

Working on it = Not working on it.

Looking into it = Can't find that file.

I'll check on that and get back to you = I'm going on vacation so it's not my problem.

It's in underwriting = We don't have a loan with that buyer's name, do we?

They're at lunch = They're not working here anymore.

They're on the other line = They're having one of their 25 smoke breaks per day and they'll be back in 40 minutes and *then* go to lunch.

The loan is approved with conditions = We just submitted to underwriting and they're on vacation.

We are waiting for loan docs = It's finally approved and we're going to Quality Control ... but they're leaving for vacation in seven minutes. Docs will be out in 2-3 short weeks.

The loan is funded! = OMG! I need approval. I told them it's been funded.

We're waiting for the wire = What escrow company are we using, anyway? Does anyone know?

QC wants to audit before we release it = We all give up and are going on vacation in seven minutes.

See? There! That was a ton of fun. Now you know how to speak LOL; it's great at cocktail parties. It's not that we don't trust loan officers ... it's more like they've SHOWN us over and over and over and over again that they cannot be trusted to know what's going on inside the buyer's loan process.

They are hoping their processers or assistants, mimes or other assorted clown staff know what's going on because they're too busy doing things I explained a couple paragraphs ago. No ... we don't trust them. They need to be constantly contacted and held to a timeline, because they have their own timelines at banks and mortgage companies and it's not OUR timeline. Most LO's don't even read the contract. Most have no idea what the cutoff day is for loan contingency, or what day it's supposed to close. There's SOFTWARE that handles this stuff ... most of them don't use it, here in 2018. Maybe they'll figure that out later ... like maybe in 2098½. Oh wait ... Just about the time they're figuring out how to use the software, the robots came by and killed everyone on earth ... soooo never mind.

We talked about this already, a reminder. Internet loans, are way more (read: much less) fun. You're working with 1-800 numbers and people without phone extensions that get transferred (read: quit) in the middle of a transaction and there's no office you can go to and speak with a manager. There's no relationship that the LO is wanting to keep with me, the agent, and the buyers and sellers, hoping for more loan referrals. None of this exists in the dark, secretive world of the Interwebs. Therefore, there's a much lower level of service and care performed by the internet robots. That's what I want … less! Who can argue with less? Internet loans will give you less everything. You're welcome!

I currently have an escrow where the mortgage broker decided to send the loan to an internet company. Let's call it Slowwwen Loans. If I had known that, we would have pulled the loan and gone elsewhere. Nope, genius lender knows best and he kept it a secret. I'm not sure what his full-time job is but it's certainly not mortgage origination. Anyway, we are currently now twenty-one days PAST close of escrow … *past* it! We still don't have the appraisal in. No one knows where it went; no one can find it. Did anyone think to call the appraiser and have him resend it? Idiocracy at its finest. We're hoping to just close the escrow, and with any extra luck have it be sometime this month instead of on the fifth, as was originally planned (it closed on the 27th).Now turn off the lights and your phone and close your eyes and imagine if that was you. As a seller OR a buyer. Grrrrrrrrr!!!!

Quoting The Grinch: "Max! Fetch me my sedative!"

CHAPTER 12

Underwriters and Other Things That Can't Live in Sunshine

"We Don't Know Where They Came From or
How to Get Rid of Them, So Let's Give Them a Job."
- Jerry Brown, governor of California*

possibly not uttered by Jerry Brown, governor, but by Gerry Browne, aluminum recycler

UNDERWRITERS HAVE NO names or faces, no business cards. They occupy offices somewhere at an unknown location, like somewhere inside the matrix, gray-green hued buildings with no signage or windows. They do not go out during the day, even the 32 smoke breaks they take ... are indoors in the underwriters' lunch room on the 32nd floor below ground. We're not sure where they came from or how they survived on earth. Their main goal is to propagate the word "NO." Their first word as youngster was "NO" and that will be their last word. As they try as hard as possible to keep up their momentum through the rest of their lives to say "NO" as many times as possible. When's the last time you were at a networking event or a cocktail party and you met an UNDERWRITER? See what I mean?

Daryl: What did the underwriter say?

LO: No.

Daryl: Why did they say no?

LO: I was afraid to ask.

Daryl: Get on the phone and ask.

LO: They said they'd follow me home if I called again.

I guess it's because they're the gatekeepers of the loot. They control all the money. There are stories that maybe they actually sit on top of piles of cash instead of using office chairs and if they actually approve a loan, their chairs would get less comfy because the pile of cash would be smaller, so they say NO. Now, that's just a possible scenario we agents came up with. The fun part lately in a Frank/Dodd environment is that the underwriters don't want to give us the entire list of documentation you need to get approved ... yes; they learned that little trick from the LOs.

"They're kind of like the Oompa Loompas of the mortgage industry."

They want to give it to you one to two pieces at a time, 10 to 35 times over. It's maddening. The LOs and processors do it like we previously discussed, but now when it goes into underwriting inside the secret cave, it will get kicked out time and again because an underwriter needs 'a little more information,' and that's when normal people go insane. It's maddening. As a seller, you ask me for an update on your buyer and their loan process. I tell you it's in underwriting. You remind me I said that last week. I remind you that underwriters are another species and you cannot upset them, or they'll follow you home. It's frustrating to share the earth with them.

The banks have made a treaty with their species and there's nothing we can do about them. They're kind of like the Oompa Loompas of the mortgage industry.

What if the buyer does not remove that loan contingency in writing once the contingency is up? Three options. Remember we talked about this? You ask them for a real-time update with real dates and figures, and maybe you give them an extension, or you cancel. This is the most frustrating part right here.

How do we handle the little things that come up? I'm asking this rhetorically.

What if the Loan Disclosures are late? There's a thing called the CD, the Certificate of Disclosure, which the lenders have to give you three days prior to close of escrow. If the Lender doesn't give you the CD three days prior, close of escrow will be delayed. When final loan approval comes, that's when the buyer removes the loan contingency. This is supposed to be completed somewhere between 10 and 21 days because that's what we negotiated in our contract.

What is that loan contingency anyway? Well, it's an "out" for a buyer if they cannot get loan approval. If they learn they cannot land the loan during the loan contingency, they can get out of the contract and get their earnest deposit back. Let's imagine that the bank actually could figure out how to do a loan from start to finish before we all die of old age. If the buyer did get final loan approval, then the buyer must remove the loan contingency in writing, assuming the buyer hasn't died of old age. Then, the buyer will do so in writing.

What does that mean? It simply means that someone over in the buyer's camp needs to know how to write simple sentences.

That means if for some reason the buyer decides not to close escrow after removing all contingencies, then the buyer may lose their earnest deposit. Now, around here, that's a big chunk of change. At $2 million, that's $60,000 because it's 3 percent of the purchase price. That's why this step is a big deal for everyone. You, the seller, want to know that your buyer can close in a timely fashion, whatever that is. Otherwise, you want to cut the cord and get back in the market because of DOM and your excitement to clean the house every day. The buyer wants to get that approval so they can move into their new shiny, beautiful house (your old, crappy house) and not lose their earnest deposit.

Also, note that if the buyer removes their loan contingency before the full loan approval and they don't get approved, they could lose all their earnest deposit. I went into a lot of detail on this because you as a seller want to know what's going on with the buyer's loan. Why are there delays? Now, you have a clue about the goings-on in Mortgage La-La Land and can understand a little more when it's time for Stupid Lender Tricks.

Me screaming into a phone: WHAT?! The buyer's loan was approved? (Loud THUD)

LO: Hello? ... Daryl? ... Hello?

Meanwhile, after I'm released from the hospital with a severe concussion, I can't remember exactly how I became a famous author.

The lender then sends the "loan package" to India or Lithuania or some other faraway place for the loan documents to be processed.

This will take a few hours to a few months, depending on the mode of transport widely used in said faraway country. Some lenders decide at this point that they need to audit this particular file, because they feel like haven't already had enough time to look at the file. They send it to loan purgatory or QC ... ah, Quality Control. It's a humorous thing, QC. It makes you wonder, why is it necessary? Is it because the rest of the operation is not really about "quality," so quality is not implied?

It's something another group of people have to do because the previous groups were all less than that? It's like when you're talking to someone and they keep saying, "I'm not lying when I say this" ... or over and over they say, "To tell you the truth" ... that's all implying that they weren't telling the truth up to that point when they pointed out that NOW... NOW is the part where I'm actually telling the truth. Up until then, who knows? It's kind of the same when they want to delay the deal another day or two for QC. Hey lenders! Do your QC while it's in underwriting and not the day we want to close, or five days after we're supposed to close.

LO: This loan has to go to QC.

Daryl: Why didn't you have QC look at it the previous 34 days you've had this file instead of waiting for today?

LO: Um, hmm ... *click*

Daryl: Hello? ... Hello? ...

> **"Daryl, it's honestly easier to build and launch satellites. I don't know how you do this day in and day out!" - Elon Musk***
> **or possibly Eon Must, hand model*

After a loan is released from loan prison (QC), the loan docs are sent to escrow, buyer will sign all 457 pages of loan docs (BTW ... do NOT expect to read these at this time). If you intend to read all the loan boiler plate, notify your lender and librarian and all the people who are saving the trees that you need to read the stuff in advance. You'll need two to three weeks to get through it and you'll need to hire a delivery truck large enough to haul all of it for you and a gaggle of beavers to cut down enough trees to print the extra paper for you to read these documents... so plan ahead.

In the olden days, the lender had to print their own documents on large printers. Imagine a large bank or mortgage company doing several hundred loans a month. All the approved loans stacked up in the printer queue. At any given time, you could have 10 to 20 loan docs in print queue in front of your buyer's docs and that could take another two days just to get them printed, because guaranteed one of those printers was going to quit working because they were all built by Xerox (I think). That could take another two days to get them printed and delivered to escrow.

Nowadays, the lender e-mails escrow the file and escrow prints it immediately. It's so much more efficient. Remember when I said the Internet changed everything? This is a place it has made a positive difference. Thank you, Al Gore!

The funniest thing a client, with an over 800 FICO score has said to me after being run through the wringer with an idiot lender doing fantastic Stupid Lender Tricks (SLT) was:

"Daryl, It's honestly easier to build and launch satellites. I don't know how you do this day in and day out!"

I laughed and reminded him... "Ummm now you know why I use sarcasm and irony in 91% of my sentences.

I went through this entire chapter, telling you all the Stupid Lender Tricks (SLT) lenders pull. All this nonsense adds up to TIME. Days and days wasted by inefficiencies. This makes most closings LATE! They couldn't CARE LESS about the closing date and you moving your stuff out and moving vans full of furniture sitting on your driveway at 5 pm on closing day, only to find out its not closing today and now at least two families are HOMELESS. Meanwhile, the processors and underwriters and document preparers are all enjoying their smoke breaks and long lunches, and are leaving early to let their cats out. And the closing is LATE. Can you see by my STRONG OVERUSE OF CAPITAL LETTERS that this stuff pisses me off beyond belief? This is why I'm writing this ... to uncover the underbelly of the idiocracies created by our lending institutions. Perhaps they should be referred to as Mental Institutions? Hmmm.

I've invited LO's and their huge staff of clowns and professional smokers to come and stand with me in the driveway in the late afternoon just after we found out we aren't closing today ... and see and feel the immense anger that's going on out on said driveway and me, with my phone in my ear, screaming something about QC. If I could ever get management to come and be there ... after they failed to perform as promised and see and hear how many people they affect w/ their carelessness and inefficiencies, and if the anger got pushed on THEM and not me ... then maybe that kind of stressful event could change something in a loan origination system to actually make it work. Yet since I'M the one on the driveway... trying to figure out a short term solution... I'M the one that gets to take the brunt of all that anger... like it's MY fault. Which it's not. UGH! Sorry for the rant ... but this is the #1 reason deals close late. And NO ONE does anything to make that work better the next time. See Definition of Insanity. I am so passionate (pissed off) about this, that I seem to produce page after page of run-on sentences.

Let's talk about Wire Fraud and Wiring Instructions. YEAH!

Did I mention selling and closing on a house is HARD? Let's talk about the current wiring instructions fraud. YEAH! Wiring instructions are sent to the buyer for the remainder of the funds to be wired into escrow at least two days prior to close of escrow; same goes for cash purchases. They're also coming to YOU, so escrow can wire you your proceeds from the sale.

Here's what's been happening. You've heard of phishing… with a PH, right? People are hacking into real estate agents' AOL, and Yahoo! and other e-mail accounts – because they're easy to hack into, I guess – and just watching and waiting until an agent has an e-mail that comes from a title company that says "wiring instructions."

Also, some agents feel like they want to send the buyers or sellers the wiring instructions instead of letting escrow do it. (It is escrow's job, by the way.) These bad people are hacking into *the agents* e-mail accounts and watching and waiting. When wire instructions show up, the hackers wait an hour or less. They've been watching your entire e-mail, so they have all the necessary e-mail addresses. They send your buyer an "updated wiring instructions" e-mail and say, "Disregard the previous e-mail; we want you to send it to this wiring place and this account number." Do you know where it's going? Offshore so it cannot be tracked. People have unknowingly wired hundreds of thousands and millions of dollars into these accounts.

They think they're wiring it into the escrow account, but instead it's going offshore and it's gone forever and it cannot be recovered. Sounds fun, right?

Currently, escrow will send you wiring instructions. It will be encrypted and it will be two-step email process. They'll send the encrypted wire instructions and you need to unencrypt them. How the heck do you unencrypt something you ask? I had to ask as well ... and then I realized it's very easily done with a medium-sized sundial, an under-ripe lemon and two rubber bands. Actually, that's not *quite* true. Escrow will send a second e-mail that will have the code to unlock the actual wiring instructions. Before they do that, they will call you and say, "I'm sending that right now." If you get a second set of wiring instructions, you call the escrow company and me. You verify that *those* are correct before you send any money, because this is a real thing. Doesn't that sound like a lot of fun? Losing all your proceeds from a multi-million-dollar sale? Let me answer for you. NO! So we're all really careful at this step.

After all of these "simple easy things" are buttoned up ... move ahead five spaces. Let's get ready for the elusive close of escrow! Again ... I'm detailing all this to show you how RIDICULOUS this whole process is and a couple other things. Real estate deals are HARD!

1. All this previous ... and forthcoming stuff I'm telling you can cause SERIOUS delays in your closing ... while I'm trying to get your deal done, so YOU can move. All these other players couldn't care less about you and your moving van in the driveway. They care more about their 21 smoke breaks, two lunch breaks, stress breaks, walking-around-the-parking-lot breaks, their vacation days and leaving at exactly 4:30 p.m. than whatever is going on over at your house ... or all of those annoying loans they're half working on.

2. CASH. This is why we L O V E Cash offers! All of these last couple of chapters and the delays and heartburn that ensue go away with a cash buyer. Just sayin'. If your deal is cash … skip Chapters 11-12. Well don't 'skip' them … read them because they're hilarious … like a typhoon inside your house. And they're hilarious, because now you can play LOL*.

*Loan Officer Lingo

Now that you've been introduced to the key players of the lending institutions, you'll be able to see the power struggle in the proper order.

1. The LO's are the only ones who are in the public eye. Therefore they have to sell, be seen in the real estate community, have to have a good reputation for closing loans on time and not overcharging or missing deadlines. They are getting barraged by the Listing Agent, Buyer's Agent, the Buyers, plus all the fun people I've mentioned previously in said institutions. They describe just about every day as 'hand to hand combat'. They fight their underwriters, appraisers, the policy makers at the bank; constantly nagging the Buyer's to get all their documentation in on time so the deal won't close late, etc. It's an all-out brawl that starts the moment a buyer makes a loan application. So much fun!

2. The appraisers are afraid of the underwriters. If the underwriter wants more documentation or another comparable sale from the appraiser, the appraiser, who isn't making a ton of money on each appraisal, has to go back and re-do the appraisal they already did. So they don't push the envelope on pricing, because they don't want to go back and re-do the appraisal because the underwriter is asking for more info.

3. The underwriters are afraid of the investors in the secondary market. They're the ones who will buy the mortgage from the bank after the bank funds the loan. (think Wall Street).

If the underwriter misses something and the investor in the secondary market doesn't want to buy that loan for whatever reason, then the bank will have to keep that debt. And said underwriter will probably get put in the time out basement on the 42nd floor below ground. Thusly, underwriters are afraid to think outside of a box when it comes to a borrower who has several properties, trusts, partnerships etc etc. They like square pegs in square holes. So they don't push the envelope when it comes down to complicated borrowers.

Yeah! It's non-stop fun down at the mental, I mean lending institution! I know what you're thinking! You're thinking that this system seems somewhat broken and is working against itself and probably needs to be re-thought and re-worked, right? Bingo! But it probably won't improve in my lifetime... maybe after the robots take control of it?

CHAPTER 13

Show Me the Money! Telling Your Neighbors You're Moving … or Not … BTW, You Should Have Moved Out By Today

D URING THIS STEP, the buyer and their agent will do a final walkthrough to make sure the house is in the same condition or better than it was when they first saw it. Also, if any repairs were needed, they want to verify they were done. If there were lots of repairs made, I want the home inspector back in to check the work. Why? Well, because he saw it and he noted it needed a repair.

He has a trained eye to know if it was repaired, and if it was done correctly or by somebody not really qualified to do the repair. I never allow non-paying parties to a walkthrough.

Accepting Advice From Strangers, Non Strangers, Strange Family Members and other Animals

A long time ago, I was doing a final walkthrough with my buyers and they brought their grumpy parents with them. Their old man was going room to room pointing out all the tiny little things that needed work. None of them were structural or anything to be concerned about, they were mostly cosmetic issues. By the time he was done critiquing the house, the buyers were crying and they canceled the deal. They really canceled. After Grumpy Dad was finished with his 'expert opinion', they were convinced the house was in terrible condition. By the way, they knew the house was an old, cheap house built in the '50s and they were excited to fix it up. Until GOM* showed up to spoil the party. *Grumpy Old Man

Do you think they lost their earnest deposit, their appraisal money, et cetera? You bet they did. They were hours from owning it. All it needed was some TLC and some paint and flooring. They knew this already. Do you think they were swayed into overreacting? You bet. Do you think they told me later that they regret it cancelling? Yes, they did. Did they wish they had their earnest deposit back? Yes, they did. Oh well! I've learned since then to not allow visitors to a walkthrough. ESPECIALLY cats or smallish rodents! You'll have to keep your Seeing Eye ferret at home.

"Recording? Dude! We finally got a recording contract? OMG!"

In some parts of the country, the act of "closing" is different. In some of the parts of the country, when you sign loan documents and have your money in escrow, they hand you the keys. In other parts of the country, "closing" implies you closing the door when you walk into the office because it's probably snowing or there's a tornado outside. This is why it's different here than in other parts of the country.

In the West, of course, we don't do that. That is what I like to call a "liability sandwich." After the buyers sign all the documents and bring in their money, escrow looks through the file and docs and makes certain everything is signed and initialed, nice and tidy. Then they send the documents back to the lender, who looks through them, make sure everything is coolio, then "funds the loan." This could be the same day or up to 2 days later, depending on the bank.

That means they wire the funds to the escrow account. Then, the go-ahead for recording is given. Recording? Dude! We finally got a recording contract? No, silly ... there's a secret place in every downtown called the 'Recorders Office.' There's no "recording equipment" or "microphones" or "guitars" there. Just County Employees milling about going on their 25 cigarette breaks and such.

Except there's a secret room with a robot that stamps Deeds and Titles to Real Estate documents as 'recorded by the county recorders (robot) office". That's a fun 'casual' explanation of the word 'recording' in this context...In a sustainable way. Nonetheless, note that the go-ahead for recordation cannot happen until the lender funds the loan and escrow gets the funds wired into their account.

*I know this is a lot to take in for most of you and it's not as detailed as much as you enginerds reading this really want. But I have to keep it light ... so I made up the part about the robots, for the non-enginerds. PLUS this terrifying to-do list is daunting to say the least. AND I've left out a lot of steps because they're more boring than the previous steps.

The title company already – hopefully – has the deed downtown at the county recorder's office waiting for the go-ahead. Once the green light is given, the county records the document. It can take a few hours to get "Confirmation of Recordation." Whew! That's a lot of spelling. Once the documents are recorded, that's closing. That's when YOU don't own that "crappy old house" anymore, and the new buyers now own the "beautiful, amazing new house." Do you see how every little step takes time? By time, I mean an extra day here, two extra days there. If my team and I aren't watching these guys like the Wil E. Coyote looking for the Road Runner, we could easily lose a day or four waiting for SLT, (Stupid Lender Tricks), or waiting for funding wires, Starbucks orders, et cetera.

If a wire isn't ordered by 11 a.m. PT, there's a chance we won't see it until the next day. What if we're trying to do this on a Friday? I NEVER intentionally close on a Friday. See the previous potential for losing a day or three, just in these last couple of steps? All of those are out of our control. That's the part that's the most frustrating for me, the parts out of our control. Ugh!

And by the way, you need to be out of the property today. Yeah, today, and all of your crap, too! Don't leave any "prizes" in the backyard or in the garage for the buyer to clean up for you. It's poor form.

You wouldn't want your previous seller's junk, or junque, still laying around for you to deal with, would you? No one likes that, so be a champ and clean up after yourself. I had some sellers a few years back who were older and had lived in their home for a long time. (Read: they hadn't sold a house and moved for a very long time.) Every time I'd go over there, I'd ask when they're going to start packing since I didn't notice any boxes around. They would say things like, "When you give me my check," and laugh. I'd remind them they need to be out by the closing day, two weeks from that day. They'd say, "Yeah, yeah." Five days from close of escrow, I went over to check their progress ... nada.

Nothing packed anywhere. I sat them down and let them know I was serious about them having five days to be out, gone, house empty. That's when they told me their neighbor – let's call him Bobby – told them they could stay for a month or so after closing. They believed Bobby and not me. WHAT?! I think they got the hint (hint???) when the buyers did their walkthrough and told the sellers they weren't closing until the sellers were out or they'd cancel three days after close of escrow had passed, then sue them for breach of contract. Then … they finally figured out that Bobby was 100 percent incorrect and I was 100 percent in the know, imagine that.

I learned to never trust that anyone really has this selling/moving thing down 100 percent and that I always need to be checking in about "moving plans." The moral of the story is to get out by COE. Depending on the condition of the place, I will have it professionally cleaned by my favorite cleaning crew. It's good karma to give the new buyer the property squeaky clean … or at least muffled-rubbing clean, unless it's a tear-down … then "just leave the couch on the porch, Clark!"

A little end-of-chapter Q&A.

Q: Can I move in before closing?

A: NO.

Q: May I stay in the house after closing?

A: NO.

Q: Should I just blindly trust that the lender is doing their job?

A: NO.

Q: Should I preemptively punch anyone I know named Bobby?

A: YES.

I make certain, in advance, that my custom For Sale sign is coming down and tell the other agent where they can pick up the keys (I usually leave the lockbox on so they can easily grab the keys and give them to their anxious buyers ... who've recently had the crap kicked out of them by SLT, LOL and robot lenders. Did you know that our current lockboxes are Bluetooth and therefore programmable? Yep. A good agent, me, (see all previous chapters) will take the time to program that blue box to the address and the MLS number of that particular listing, because No. 1, it will give me showing stats of the property by week and by month, and No. 2, I get an e-mail every time one of my lockboxes is opened with the date, time, address, agent name, company phone and e-mail. Plus I can play my Spotify and wirelessly operate a waffle iron as well!

Every time a box is opened, I know who's been there and when it happened. If I take the extra time to program that bad boy, I have another level of security to know if anyone's in the house and if I gave them permission to use that box. You probably cannot imagine this, but some agents are careless and lazy and don't check to see if the house is occupied or vacant or has an alarm or if it's in escrow. Some agents see a box and a sign and "assume" they can wander on in. If an unauthorized person does that to my lockboxes, oh man, there's going to be a problem. I'm VERY protective of my people.

After closing, you'll get the proceeds of the sale wired to you. Remember the extra caution to use when wiring? Then the buyer gets the keys and I'm at the point where I'm nearly done with my job.

By the way... CONGRATS!!! Yippee! This is when we break out the champagne!

CHAPTER 14

Why I Need My Head Examined

THAT'S IT! SEE how easy that was? BTW ... its way more complicated than this. There are several more moving parts that I didn't even mention. When you're inside of a transaction ... some days you wonder if you'll ever get out of it with your hair and sanity intact. Look at me, I look like hell and I'm only 27*. Whoa.

*anteater years

By the way, if you're reading this, thank you for getting all the way to the end of this book. You're much smarter than when you started and it shows. You even look smarter!

Back to what we haven't talked about ... well ... barely.

I've done ALL OF THE ABOVE without being paid to do it! Say what?

I've borne 100 percent of the marketing costs, inspections, photos, house cleaners, and videos. I've employed others to help and paid them myself, spent countless hours of my time and my team's time, all without any guarantee of being paid. If your house never sold, I'd be out all of it and it would be a total loss. Would you be interested in running that kind of business?

We make 100 percent of our income on commission. There's no salary or guaranteed paycheck on the 1st and 15th. This is why I show up at your door, with this complicated marketing strategy and centuries* of market knowledge and knowhow. What we do for you is pretty damn spectacular without asking for any upfront cash or any guarantee. The only "guarantee" is when we get a buyer and everyone jumps through all the hoops listed above (plus about 967 more that aren't mentioned here for boredom's sake) and the deal closes. Then and only then do I get a paycheck. Some of us are just born as people who love to serve. We're givers. Think about this… you work 8am-6pm, let's say, and you're too busy to read all my emails and texts about your lender doing SLT (*Stupid Lender Tricks). You get home and you're tired … spouse, kids, dinner, homework etc. You catch up on the Clown Car Antics of the mortgage industry for the day and you call me for a recap. What time is that? 8? 9? 10pm? Of COURSE I'm still working… right? I need to be available 24 hours a day… right? If I don't pick up… you're mad at me for not being 'available'… no matter what time it is or what day it is. Sounds relaxing…right? See previous… we're givers. We love to help people and to serve. (And we're all suffering from some sort of brain damage) Don't call me after 9…

I get a kick out of all this creative thinking and implementation and watching a plan work. At the same time, I'm always looking for more efficient, creative ways to do things, things to up my High Touch Concierge Service (HTCS). I'm always changing, always wanting to do it better and to make the process less stressful and more fun for you. Plus I'm constantly trying to outwit and outrun SLT and LOL. (Stupid Lender Tricks and Loan Officer Lingo) I just love helping you plan from start to finish. Devise the plan and run it. That's just me.

When you're ready to sell and if you're in the South Bay, near LAX, you need me. I need you. Call, write, text. I'll buy you coffee or DM you on Insta, whatever works for you. I want to be the one that helps you get from Pointe A to Pointe B. Besides that ... we all know you need me.

I can't remember if I mentioned this yet, so stop me if I did. I'll leave you with this short poem:

Real Estate deals are HARD.

It's hard to park on Bard.

If you'd like to send a fax, press the star key.

A poem by Daryl Palmer

ENDTRODUCTION

I Know You Are... But What Am I?

WHO AM I? A dad, a grandfather, a brother ... Bobby is my brother (see Glossary of Terms), a lover, a beach cruiser, a chocoholic, a connector, a wine evangelist, musician, a beach lover, a recovering long-distance runner, a someone always recovering from some injury, sock hater, and an outside-the-box thinker. I'm fun, lighthearted, sarcastic, (what?) knowledgeable, intuitive, creative, and EXTREMELY LOYAL. My "thing" is keeping things light. I'm hilarious all of the time (just ask me) and I'm serious when I need to be. Inside a real estate transaction, I'm LASER focused. Oh yeah ... I've also been selling real estate full time since 1986. (See "grandfather" above. I'm an old dude ... I just don't act like one.)

Where do I live? I grew up in NorCal, Sacramento ... a great place to be *from*, and I got OUT. I went to college in San Diego in the '70s, and that's when I discovered SoCal. They didn't talk much about it in NorCal other than making a list: Traffic, smog, and crazy people. Not much has changed since then except the air. The first time I came to the LA Basin in the mid '70s, the air – the sky? Whatever – was purple and orange, except it wasn't even close to sunset. The smog was so bad back then, I never saw the San Gabriel Mountains just to the east of LA towering over the valley. I had no idea they were there until years later when they started cleaning up the polluters.

When I first saw the mountains, I was surprised that they were there and so close. In the winter, there can be snow on top ... think Big Bear. But NO ONE in NorCal EVER talked about the weather in SoCal.

NorCal = four seasons. SoCal = two seasons.

Season one, doors open. Long season.

Season two, doors closed. Short season.

The Ocean and the sand and the mild weather. It was then I realized I was a beach kid. You either hate the ocean and the sand or you love it. I love, love, love two seasons. I love the South Bay, it's so close to LAX and LA and everything. Yet the beach cities – Manhattan Beach, Hermosa Beach and Redondo Beach – are still quaint beach towns, all with a small-town feel.

It's an amazing place surrounded by all the chaos of the LA Basin. The people are friendly and laid back. The beaches are amazing strands of sand and surf. The real estate is interesting because every house is unique ... no tract homes here. It's a wonderful and exciting place to be. Small-town warning! This area is tiny, even though we're less than five miles from LAX we are still a small town, baby! People from the Westside come here and notice we're different here. We're laid back at the beach. It's totally a beachy vibe. We dress how we want, and we all want to be comfy so that means shorts and flip-flops as often as possible.

My broker is a bit more old-school than me; he wears a tie every day. He keeps telling me to stop wearing shorts. I remind him we're selling a lifestyle here. Ahem! We live at the beach ... remember? The Big, Blue Wet Thing! A lot of millionaire and billionaire surfers are out there on the water. We all look the same in a wetsuit or board shorts. I dress like everyone else. However, if you're wearing a tie AND a jacket, you could be accused of being a Westsider, aka a "Westy," a lawyayer, Mortgage Big Shot or a wig salesman. It's OK …we're laid back here. It's the beach, baby! This is why I love this place!!! I love how friendly people here are. They will go out of their way to converse with you and are happy to help. It's an amazing part of earth. People who grew up here, never left. Where else would you go? Hawaii is beautiful, but you could end up with island fever. Where else has our weather and our big, blue wet thing including the beautiful beaches and amazing surfing?

Those are just some of the reasons I love where I live. If you live here, you know. Either way, call me. I can help you find the perfect home here. You already know I can sell your house!

Find photos of where I live and what I do on Instagram @itsabeachything. Find me on Facebook at *Daryl Palmer Beach Homes*. Also on Facebook at *Best Of South Bay and Instagram* @thebestofsouthbay, where I interview local businesses and we all have fun doing it.

Thanks for listening. Now go have a martini!

Daryl Palmer CRS

310-502-4240

Daryl@DarylPalmer.com

RE/MAX Estate Properties

#01986622

GLOSSARY OF TERMS: SOME REAL, SOME DARYLISMS... WHICH ARE ALSO REAL

Anteater Years   No one really knows what this is.

AVRs   Automatic Valuation Robots. They know less than you (and they) think. Except they're wrong 90% of the time ... not that that means anything to you. But it does...or doesn't.

The Bobby's   Bobby is Daryl's brother, and therefore Daryl wanted to mention his beloved brother, Bobby, as many times as possible, even to the point of ridiculousness. Which is exactly what happened. Only because Daryl and his son Nate* published their books before Bobby (see: The Bobby's) did, even though Bobby was the first one to start writing his book. None of that has anything to do with anything except I, Daryl, just wanted to point it out. *Nate published first

COE   Close of Escrow, also Cursing Often Everyday.

Comps   Comparable Sales in the neighborhood. Also, what we want the chef to do when we're eating at Arthur J's. See also: Jazz Piano.

Darylisms   Hillarious* things that Daryl thinks up (*or possibly not hilarious)

Docator	See Lawyayer.
DOM	Days On Market; No one's friend, ever. Unless you're a buyer in a crappy market. AKA: Bitch.
GOM	Grumpy Old Man. AKA: Bitch.
Handful Of Years	"We're still waiting to hear back from underwriting."
HTCS	High Touch Concierge Service. Daryl's term used to define what he does to help you get a property sold. Part of his Marketing Suite. Also: PPF and OTB.
Insanity	Expecting to get a loan from a lending institution and have it be seamless and efficient and on time. See: Cursing Often Everyday (COE).
Interwebs	AKA Interpol. Something about 007 Spies. Possible British play on words for any word starting with "Inter" See: Interchangeable.
Lawyayer	See: Realader
Legal Fart Jargon	Something about your grandfather farting in a chair.
Liability Sandwich	When you create extra liability for yourself. Almost like a Knuckle Sandwich, but it includes Lawyayers and a nice Aioli w/ arugula… In a Sustainable Way

Loan Officer	Someone you'll most likely not invite to any parties you may have
LOL	A fun game called Loan Officer Lingo, played at many parties worldwide
NAR	Not Always Rhinoceros' … also National Association of Realtors
OTB	Outside-the-Box thinking. The "NON-Cul-de-sac" Daryl lives in
Overdressus Maximus	Bankers, Lawyayers or Westies
PPF	Pre-Planning Fun. The Real way to sell your house and make more $$$!
Realtor	A TWO-syllable word describing the professional association real estate agents join. The National Association of Realtors (NAR) is the largest trade organization in the U.S.
Realater/ Realader	Idiot posing as a professional real estate agent. DO NOT HIRE these people!
Real Estate Officer	A name Daryl made up to make fun of the term 'Loan Officer' and is actually considering keeping it for himself. Officer Daryl. AKA: Officer.

Recordation   When the robot in the secret room in the Recorders Office officially 'stamps' the documents to show the home ownership has changed. **See also:** COE.

Robots   They do not exist anywhere (said the robot trying to take over the world).

SBLAMP   South Bay Lazy Agent Marketing Plan

SLT   Stupid Lender Tricks. Things Lenders do to prolong your agony whilst trying to obtain a home loan and pay for their boat in King Harbor.

WWDD?   What Would Daryl Do? This is always an interesting and potentially scary question. (read: amazing). See Darylisms.

Zillowed, Zilly etc.   Words Daryl uses to define getting possibly and unknowingly tricked by AVRs. (See: Automatic Valuation Robots).

Children's Miracle Network and Children's Hospital LA

How did I get involved with Children's Miracle Network and Children's Hospital LA?

RE/MAX got involved with CMN somewhere in the late 80s or early 90s. My youngest was born in stress and was on a ventilator for the first month of her life in a Children's Hospital that was involved with CMN, so I started donating a portion of my commissions to CMN in the names of my clients. It was a little thing. And we've done CMN fundraisers at the RE/MAX office. But I always wanted to do a bit more.

Then I was invited to an open house at CHLA. It's the top Children's Hospital in California. They see more than 500,000 patients every year! We got to see the kid's library. Yes they have a library! And for every 20 minutes a child is in the library reading, they give them a free book. Do you have any idea how many books they give away at CHLA each year? A TON! These cannot be used books, because of germs, etc. They're all new books. All donated. They give away more than 50,000 books to kids at that hospital per year! It's a tiny room, but it's a book-giving machine!

Some stats:

374 beds

106 pediatric critical care beds

More than 500,000 patient visits per year

More than 88,000 ER visits per year

More than 16,000 pediatric surgeries per year

More than 16,000 inpatient admissions per year

More than 2,300 patients transported by helicopter, Lear jet and ambulance

They do not turn down anyone who comes there! That's the biggest thing!

To top it off, they also have a large blood bank and need more than 200 units donated per WEEK!

This is a place my heart goes out to. All those terrified kids and their terrified parents. Not knowing the outcome. Day after day in that hospital. Clinging to doctors and nurses comments, phone calls that wake you in the middle of the night. Constant staring and studying the monitors, watching for changes. The nonstop beeping of the monitors and the alarms that scare the crap out of you. This is where my heart is. I've been there. I've been that parent, trying to be strong and yet terrified if your kid will be ok. It's been over 25 years since I lived in the hospital like that and I'm still highly emotional about that experience and that part of my own family's lives.

I'm crying right now as I write this, because it still has a strong pull on my heart and my memory of her birth and her long stay in NICU. It's a deep thing man!

So I give and try to make others aware of the needs that these Children's Hospitals have. It's not a "tax write off". It's extremely personal.

If you are interested in knowing more or helping out or even taking a tour of the hospital to see it first hand, I can help you arrange it. I'll probably join you. Because this is heavy stuff man!

CHLA & CMN.

Whoa.

You can call me at 310-502-4240. Or email me at Daryl@ DarylPalmer.com. We can talk about getting you over there & see for yourself what's going on.

They REALLY make a difference in the South Bay! It's an amazing place!

Now SERIOUSLY… go make that martini!

www.ingramcontent.com/pod-product-compliance
Lightning Source LLC
Chambersburg PA
CBHW022106210326
41520CB00045B/398